IMAGES OF LONDON

NORWOOD PUBS

IMAGES OF LONDON

NORWOOD PUBS

JOHN COULTER

TEMPUS

First published 2006

Tempus Publishing Limited
The Mill, Brimscombe Port,
Stroud, Gloucestershire, GL5 2QG
www.tempus-publishing.com

British Library Cataloguing in Publication Data.
A catalogue record for this book is available from the British Library.

ISBN 0 7524 3837 9

Typesetting and origination by Tempus Publishing Limited.
Printed in Great Britain.

CONTENTS

J. E. ABRAHAMS

Ye Olde Holly Bush Hotel

WESTOW HILL, UPPER NORWOOD.

SPECIAL DINNERS, 1/-   TEAS, ETC., ETC.

Open Sundays 12.30 to 2.30, and 6 to 10.

"Signs of the Times at Norwood."

BY JOE LYNCH.

A friend and I went out one day,
  Looking smart and bold,
We called at **"Ye Olde Gipsy House,"**
  Our fortunes to have told ;
We climbed **"2 Towers"** with **"Hamilton Arms"**
  Though Morgan's **"Bricklayers"** were near ;
We had a chat with **"Paxton"** then,
  And drank his sparkling beer ;
There's **"Colby"** standing with **"George the Fourth"**
  Just near **"The Gipsy Hotel,"**
We heard **"The Duke of Cornwall"**
  Ringing Morgan's **"Railway Bell"** ;
Just then we saw **"The Woodman"**
  Looking towards the **"Swan"** ;
"The Cambridge" and **"The Oxford"**
  Were putting their colours on.
My friend, he quite admired them,
  And gloried in their charms,
With Dawson comfortably seated
  In good old **"Brunswick's Arms"** ;
We called and had a jolly chat
  Over a glass of bitter and bun,
And when we got out of **"The Thicket"**
  We saw **"The Rising Sun."**
Again we met dear old **"Paxton,"**
  A man of skills and mights,
And bidding him a very good day
  We climbed the **"Alma"** heights.
"The White Hart" on the Westow track
  Was making such a rush,
We saw him hide his shiny back
  In Abraham's **"HOLLY BUSH."**
We met **"Royal Albert,"** who wore a **"Crown,"**
  With all his ma's and pa's ;
We felt so tired, so we settled down
  Inside **"The Holborn Bars."**

An Edwardian rhymed celebration of the pubs of Upper and West Norwood. Of those mentioned the Thicket Hotel in Anerley Road is the only one excluded from this book. (John Gent)

INTRODUCTION

Norwood is unusual in being a suburb that was created almost entirely from scratch at the beginning of the nineteenth century, on land that had formerly been open common. As a result it had only three or four pubs in the eighteenth century, the Horns and the Rose & Crown on the edge of the common, plus the Old Gipsy House and perhaps the Goat House sheltering in permitted encroachments on the common itself. The task for the Norwood pub historian is therefore to chronicle the modest growth between 1800-50, and the explosion in numbers in the high-Victorian period. Norwood was then seriously over-supplied with pubs and hotels. This book gives details of more than 100 of which less than half survive. In addition there were numerous beerhouses that have been excluded because their names, and often their addresses, have not been recovered.

Why were there so many pubs? The demand must obviously have been greater than it is today, probably because the home lives of most Victorians were even more dismal than our own. The history of the Norwood pubs illustrates another reason for this multiplication, in the love affair of so many Victorian builders with the idea of innkeeping. In this book the reader will find countless examples of pubs being run by the men who built them. In several cases it is explicitly stated that they had retired to keep the pubs of their own creation. Given that the establishment of a new one was a risky business, because of the uncertainty of obtaining a full licence, many of these men must have been obsessed with a Dickensian vision of the jolly life of 'mine host' that was far removed from the sordid realities of a landlord's life in a London suburb.

Lower (or West) Norwood, as the oldest and poorest part of the district, had the highest concentration of pubs. The drinking habits of Lower Norwood, and the plentiful supply of places in which to indulge them, are suggested by this evidence from an 1875 inquest, in which the elderly witness describes taking a walk with his wife and meeting a total stranger:

> We were passing the Gipsy Queen public house, and he stood at the door. He accosted us, and asked us if we would have something to drink. I said, 'Thank you, Sir, I will, please,' and we went in. He called for a quarten of gin and some beer between the three of us. From there we went to the Hope and had some more, and after that we went to the Thurlow. He called for something there, but they would not serve him. I and my wife were sober, but at the Thurlow they appeared to refuse him because he was the worse for drink. Then from there we went to the Horns. He there called for another pot of beer, which we had between us. It was a pot of fourpenny ale. He said he would have something else, and I think he had half a quarten of neat gin.

Authority had long been anxious about this over-production of pubs, and magistrates had tried to keep it in check by issuing new licences sparingly. But as more brewers joined the bench this restraint became less effective. Between 1830-69 the magistrates had no control over the establishment of a newly invented type of pub, the beerhouse. From 1872 new legislation gave them some power to close superfluous pubs, and the 1904 Licensing Act made this much easier by creating a compensation fund. As a result, numbers fell throughout the twentieth century, with the backstreet corner pub becoming increasingly rare. After 1989 the enforced break-up of the brewers' tied estates turned the gentle decline into an avalanche, so that at times while researching this book I have feared that Norwood's pubs would soon require the attention of an archaeologist more than a chronicler.

Fixing the boundaries of such an amorphous district as Norwood must always be a subjective exercise. I have tended to be inclusive, reaching as far south as the Railway Tavern at Woodside, north to the Tulse Hill Hotel, and east to the Rosendale Hotel. To the west there was no difficulty of choice, as the debatable ground between Norwood and Streatham is singularly dry. I have excluded most of the many wine bars and licenced restaurants that have sprung up in the relaxed climate of the last thirty years, and also most of Norwood's recently founded hotels.

This is intended as a work of reference. I would strongly advise against attempting to read it from cover to cover, as I have no wish to be responsible for boring anyone to death. In general the history of one Victorian pub is likely to be much like that of the next, so it is hard to give much variety to concise accounts of 100.

Because they nearly always return to them eventually, I have listed all the pubs under their traditional names rather than their trendy and transient modern ones. A list of alternative pub names, old and new, will be found on p.125.

The scope of the work has not made it possible to list all the landlords and landladies. Some pubs had a different one almost every year, especially in the late nineteenth century. Nor have I attempted, in most cases, to trace the names of the licensees after the directories ceased to give them in 1959. Instead, I have mentioned the notable figures at each pub, the celebrities and those who have remained in charge for a long time. All the landlords and ladies included will be found in the index on p.126.

ACKNOWLEDGMENTS AND PICTURE CREDITS

My thanks to the following for generous help and advice: Mrs Jill Farmer, John Gent, Jerry Savage at Upper Norwood Joint Library, Steve Roud and Chris Bennett at Croydon Local Studies Library, Len Riley and Graham Gower at Lambeth Archives, and Simon Finch and Elizabeth Silverthorne at Bromley Local Studies Library.

I am grateful to Mrs Jill Farmer, John Gent, Lambeth Archives, Croydon Local Studies Library and Upper Norwood Joint Library for the use of illustrations.

The other illustrations are from my own collection.

Norwood Pubs – an A-Z

THE ALBERT, No.67 HARRINGTON ROAD

David Bowker, who had opened the Albert as a beerhouse, probably in 1867, applied for a full licence early in 1868, but was refused. Bowker was a builder as well as a publican, so it is likely that the Albert was his own creation. The name was presumably in honour of the Prince Consort, who had died in 1861, but the Prince of Wales (much to his disgust) was also an Albert, and he had been married rather more recently. Having failed to secure a licence, Bowker sold or let the beerhouse to Nathaniel Barton Cook, an experienced publican who had run the Selhurst Arms for seven-and-a-half years. The magistrates were better pleased with him, and granted a licence in 1870. The original building has been described as 'a really old cottagey type pub and a very popular place'. It was popular, no doubt, certainly with the landlords who tended to stay for a long time, but 'cottagey' seems inaccurate. The only known photograph shows a substantial three-storey corner pub.

The long-serving landlords were George Hope from 1898-1923, and Frederick C. Whittle from 1924 until the Second World War. The Albert was destroyed by a flying bomb in 1944 with the loss of seven lives, and not rebuilt until 1965-66. This is an extraordinarily long delay even for a pub, a type of building that had a low priority in the post-war pecking order. During the 1990s the owners found the secret of instant unpopularity by changing the name to the Pickled Newt. The locals naturally refused to make use of the name or, in many cases, of the pub. As a proof that even a brewer can eventually see the light, the sign is now the Albert Tavern once more.

THE ALBION, No.26 SOUTH NORWOOD HIGH STREET

The Albion was built on the prime corner site of Pascall's brick fields, which had closed in 1864 when the lease expired. The pub was opened as a beerhouse by James Clement Phelps by March 1867, when he first applied for a full licence. Phelps described the pub as 'a nobly constructed' house, of which he had taken a twenty-one year lease. In 1869 the rear parts of the building became the first South Norwood Fire Brigade station, and this respectable connection was useful in persuading the magistrates to grant the licence in 1870. A fireman, after all, might often need a dram to stiffen his nerve. Phelps remained until 1872, in which year the pub was described as the Albion Arms. The longest-serving of his successors were George Edward Fage from 1888-1909

The first Albert Tavern, c.1910. (Croydon Local Studies Library)

The second Albert Tavern, when known as the Pickled Newt, in 1998.

The Albion, c.1914. (John Gent)

and Walter Ernest Marriott from 1935 until the mid-1950s. Two of the more transient landlords had unusual names: there was George Samuel Pummell in 1910 and Percy Watts Figgess in 1913. Thomas James Harding had two spells in charge, from 1914-17 and from 1921-24, which were perhaps separated by military service. The Albion is now one of several pubs that represents itself as the local for Crystal Palace FC supporters.

THE ALEXANDRA, NO.1 HURLSTONE ROAD

This possible pub was built in 1887 by Thomas Gibbons, the developer of Alexandra (now Hurlstone) Road. It had three tenants in the first two years: Charles William Jenkins, George Walker and Ernest Hugh Gough Stevens. Peter Walker says that it was a pub from 1887-89, before becoming an off-licence, but the late 1880s rate books call it a house and shop, and the directories give it either as a grocer's shop or as a, 'grocer and beer retailer'. It seems more likely that it was a grocer's shop with an off-licence from the start. It is now a house.

THE ALEXANDRA HOTEL, NOS 21 AND 23 CLIFFORD ROAD

Although Norwood Junction opened in 1859, the race to provide South Norwood's commuters with liquid refreshment close to the new station did not hot up until the mid-1860s. Both the Alliance and the South Norwood Railway Hotel (now the Cherry Tree) were built in 1864-65. They were launched successfully, and still flourish today. The spectacular loser in the race was the Alexandra Hotel (named after the new Princess of Wales) which was built at the same time in Clifford Road, then Lower Station Road, on the other side of the railway tracks.

The former Alexandra in 2006.

Above left: The former Alexandra Hotel in 2002.

Above right: The Alliance Tavern, *c.*1914.

Building a new public house was a serious gamble at that period. The magistrates, who were always reluctant to grant a new licence, could sometimes be softened if the new house was sufficiently large and expensive. But if the speculator spent huge sums on his intended pub and could still not get it licenced he was liable to be left heavily in debt and saddled with a building ill-suited for other uses. That was the fate of the Alexandra Hotel's owners. The first application in 1866 was refused because the intended houses in the surrounding streets had not yet been built. A second application failed because the hotel itself was not complete. The Alexandra had opened meanwhile as a beerhouse, but that was not a viable use for such a large building. When further applications for a full licence failed in 1869 and 1870 the projectors gave up hope, and the pub was closed around 1873 after an inglorious career of eight years or less. It was subsequently used as a furniture repository, as the Crown Coffee Palace, as a laundry, as a Good Templars' Lodge, etc. It is now divided into offices.

THE ALLIANCE TAVERN, NO.91 SOUTH NORWOOD HIGH STREET

The Alliance was built around 1864 and opened as a beerhouse by Charles Churney. What was the alliance commemorated by the name? Most likely the marriage of the Prince of Wales and Princess Alexandra of Denmark in 1863, an event that also gave a name to the rival establishment, the Alexandra Hotel, across the railway tracks. Those two and the South Norwood Railway Hotel were the pubs built to compete for the commuter trade after Norwood Junction was opened in 1859. The first application for a full licence for the Alliance was made by Alfred Holder in 1867. That was not successful, but one had been obtained by 1878, when the new owner Henry Laver advertised the pub as the Alliance Wine & Spirit establishment. The only long-serving landlord was Robert Cecil Coy, who was in charge from 1909-36.

The Alma in 1995.

THE ALMA TAVERN, NO.95 CHURCH ROAD

This pub, which was built between 1854-60, was named after the Battle of the Alma in the Crimean War, which was fought on 20 September, 1854. The most likely building date is 1855-56. Alma Road was being used as an alternative name for Fox Hill by 1856, which is probably an indication that the pub existed, although the road name could have come directly from the battle. The first publican may have been John Walker, who in March 1856 was granted a licence 'for a house at Westow Hill, Penge'. At that time 'Westow Hill' was often used to mean Church Road and the Triangle, and it was certainly given as part of the Alma's address in 1860. Wilson says incorrectly that 'the Alma public house was half in Croydon and half in Penge. It is licenced by Penge.' Maps show the whole pub in the district of Penge, now part of Bromley, with only the pavement outside in Croydon.

   The first ascertained landlord is Robert Harvey May who was installed by 1860 and remained until 1863. One of his early successors, Robert Blackshaw, landlord in the late 1860s, was often in the news for the wrong reasons: being involved in a fight, receiving a reprimand for allowing out of hours drinking, etc. The other Victorian licensees did not stay long, and made little mark for good or bad. The history of the Alma in the first half of the twentieth century was dominated by Lilian Perry, who came to the pub as a barmaid around 1906, promptly married Steve Swain, the landlord, and took over the licence when he died in 1927. A couple of years later she married a Mr Mason ('a Plymouth man'), was widowed again in 1953, and was still running the pub in 1958. Since 1937 her son-in-law had been joint licensee.

THE AUCKLAND TAVERN, NO.103 GIPSY ROAD

This was another pub that proved an utter failure. The building, of three storeys, with a parapet, existed by 1870, but if it ever opened for business it was only briefly or intermittently. The lease was offered for sale in 1889 and again in 1892. On the second occasion it was described as

The remains of the former
Auckland Tavern in 2004.

'business premises known as the Auckland Tavern, suitable for a coffee tavern, boarding house, or for business premises requiring ample space'. The ground floor became a shop and the upper rooms were made available for other uses. In 1899 and 1900 the Gipsy Road Tabernacle held 'a Sunday school with Bible classes at Auckland Tavern, formerly a public-house, where also during the week various agencies were conducted'. The building survived the Second World War. The flats now on the site seem to incorporate some of the fabric of the old pub.

THE BEEHIVE, NO.47 WOODSIDE GREEN

The Beehive was built in 1844, on a fresh site. The first occupant was the owner, and probably the builder, one R. Rogers. He soon began to let it to tenants, John Williams 1846-47, Edward Moore 1848-49, T. Wilding 1850-51, William James Legg (or Legge) 1852-55, and then to John Wood. The Beehive was operated as a beerhouse until 1852, when Legg obtained a full licence. The Shirley brewer John Murton, who already held a lease, bought the freehold for £525 in 1859. That price included a three-acre meadow with an ornamental pond. The pub was described as:

> That desirable country inn known as the Bee Hive, with seven bedrooms, parlour, bar parlour, bar, kitchen - partly used as a provision shop, good cellarage, etc.; coach house, carriage yard, skittle alley, piggery, etc. There is an attractive Tea Garden filled with shrubs, and forming a shady Summer Retreat.

John Wood was then paying Murton a rent of £47 per annum.

In the early years, when Woodside was still a sleepy village, there was apparently not enough business to sustain a mere drinking shop, so several of the early publicans had second strings to their bows. In the 1850s and 1860s John Wood used the tea garden to attract the jaunting trade, and in the 1870s his widow Elizabeth Wood was described as a licenced victualler and wood

The Beehive
in 1895.
(John Gent)

The Beehive
in 2003.

broker. The longest-serving licensees were Selsby Hunt Catterson, who was here for thirty years, from 1880-1909, and Mrs Amelia Jessie Beeston from 1910-24. The building is a locally listed which is perhaps more a sentimental tribute to the Beehive's long history than a sober assessment of its current architectural quality. The most prominent feature is now the second storey built over the old bars, probably in the 1930s, and entirely at odds with the style of the rest of the pub. Not that it was ever a thing of beauty; just a plain square house, with a forecourt until the single-storey bars were built out to the street after 1868.

The Beulah Retreat, Beulah Hill

This short-lived beerhouse, first heard of in 1858, was on the site of some additional stables of the Beulah Spa Hotel, which stood diagonally opposite the hotel on what is now the eastern corner of Harold Road. The pub probably reused the old stableman's cottage. There had been an opening for a simple beerhouse for servants in Beulah Hill since the Royal Oak was closed in the 1850s, especially as the Beulah Spa Tap was being rebuilt at the same time. The problem for small businesses in this high-class residential area was that their sites were liable to be required for redevelopment at any time, and that was the fate that awaited the Beulah Retreat, which closed in 1865. Although the houses that replaced it, Nos 32 and 34 Beulah Hill, were not built for a decade, it was probably impossible for a beerhouse to obtain a fresh lease for such a potentially valuable site.

The nurseryman W.G. Pringle's earliest recollection of Beulah Hill was 'that it was a very narrow lane with a few shops, houses, and beerhouses, one of which was known as the Beulah Retreat; it was here that local people obtained their beer and butter'. Mrs Dee, describing Beulah Hill as she first knew it in 1858, mentions:

> The Beulah Retreat, a funny little straggling cottage, I am not sure how many rooms it had, but it was all on one floor, this was kept as a beerhouse by Mr Isaac Smith, who afterwards kept the Eagle Public House in New Town, when the Beulah Spa Tap was finished and opened by Mr Preddy.

Isaac Smith was at the Eagle by 1859, and William Preddy at the Beulah Spa Tap by 1861. Mrs Dee presumably means that Smith chose not to struggle against this imminent competition. The next recorded landlord was James Corn, who was listed in 1860, but for the rest of its brief

The Beulah Spa in 1998.

existence the Beulah Retreat was run by George Hunt, who went on to greater things as the founder of the Conquering Hero.

THE BEULAH SPA, NOW HARVESTER, NO.41 BEULAH HILL

The existing Beulah Spa pub ought perhaps to be considered merely as a continuation of the Tap, but as it was rebuilt soon after the hotel was demolished in 1937, and as it has grown to take over part of its role, there is some justification for treating it as a new foundation. Charrington's seized the opportunity to use part of the site of the hotel to make their pub larger than the old Tap, no doubt with the hope of inheriting some of the hotel's reputation and custom. The new pub opened in October 1939, with John Hart from the Tap as the first landlord. J.B. Wilson, writing in the 1940s, thought the rebuilding was along 'very modern lines'. Hart remained until 1955. The main events since his day have been the addition of a Toby restaurant on the west side of the pub in 1988-89, and the extensive alterations made in the spring of 1996, when the Beulah Spa was converted into a Harvester restaurant. The historic name has now been entirely suppressed in favour of Harvester.

THE BEULAH SPA HOTEL, NO.43 BEULAH HILL

John Davison Smith, the founder of the Beulah Spa pleasure grounds, blundered sadly by not thinking about hotel accommodation for his visitors until it was too late. In December 1831 he advertised a first-rate hotel to be let near the Beulah Spa, where one 'is in great requisition … the house is large and commodious and admirably adapted for the purpose.' This was almost

The Beulah Spa Hotel *c.*1860, with the Crystal Palace imaginatively relocated. (Croydon Local Studies Library)

Beulah Spa, Upper Norwood.   A.S. 3046

certainly the Old Spa House, No.249 South Norwood Hill (where Spa Close is now), which was the only large house in the vicinity occupied by Smith at that time. The Old Spa House was too far from the London entrance of the pleasure grounds to make an ideal hotel, and in any case Smith had missed the boat. By October 1831 an enterprising rival, James Fielding, had built and opened the Beulah Spa Hotel directly opposite the main gate. Smith continued to bluster. Advertisements for the Beulah Spa mention stabling within the grounds and stress that it has 'no connection with the Spa Hotel or stabling without the gates', but there were no takers for the offered Old Spa House hotel lease, and Smith was reduced to running it as a mere boarding house. By 1834 he was a bankrupt, his whole Beulah Spa project in ruins.

James Fielding, meanwhile, was prospering at the parasitic Beulah Spa Hotel, which he operated until his death in 1851, and left to his widow. Fielding had worked on a large scale from the first, evidently renting far more land than he needed for his immediate purposes. In March 1832 he advertised fifty to 100 acres at Norwood as being available to any gentleman desirous of country recreation, by which he presumably meant shooting. In July 1842 Fielding advertised that he had 'greatly extended his premises by taking in the adjoining house, and can now offer the combined comforts of a public and private hotel'. This acquisition was Spa Cottage, half of a semi-detached pair to the west, which had an on-and-off relationship with the hotel during the nineteenth century before being replaced by the new ball and concert room in the 1890s. In 1849 Fielding added what was variously described as a large room or a large wing to the hotel. This may have been the single storey wing to the east, parallel with Spa Hill, but it is equally possible that it was something that did not survive the extensive alterations made a decade later.

Fielding's death in 1851 spared him the troubles that inevitably came upon the hotel with the arrival of the Crystal Palace and the final ruin of the Beulah Spa pleasure grounds. His widow, Eliza Ann, remained for only a couple of years before selling to the ubiquitous Thomas Masters of the Royal Crystal Palace Hotel. He ran the Beulah Spa Hotel for a while in tandem with his other enterprises, but in the summer of 1854, with his finances crumbling, he was

Opposite: The Beulah Spa Hotel, front view, *c.*1910.

Right: The Beulah Spa Tap, *c.*1910. (Upper Norwood Joint Library)

trying to sell either the freehold or a lease. His advertisements described it, rather desperately, as 'to a man of spirit a decided fortune'. The purchaser was one Goodwin, who was at the Beulah Spa Hotel in 1855. By the next year it was empty. This was the great crisis in its history, for when it re-emerged in 1859 it had a new proprietor, a new function, a new name, and a new building.

The new master was Lewis A. Ritterbrandt, MD, physician, or Louis Antoine Ritterbrandt as he was called on the twenty-eight year lease he took in June 1859. He was the front man for a limited company formed to rebuild and run the hotel. The new function was to be a health resort for jaded Victorians, and the new name was the Beulah Spa Hydropathic Institution and Hotel. The building was probably only partially new. The three-storey central section may well have been Fielding's original hotel of 1831, in which case the late 1850s work consisted of the matching two-storey wings on either side. To make room for the western wing it was necessary to move the stables and Tap to the corner of Spa Hill. Ritterbrandt's rent of £600 per annum must have required him to fill most of his thirty bedrooms most of the time. With numerous rival hotels in Norwood, and even a rival hydro at Sydenham, this cannot have been easy, especially as Ritterbrandt was moonlighting three days a week at a Turkish bath in Chancery Lane. By November 1861 he, or more likely his creditors, had despaired, and the lease and the 'nearly new and superior furniture' were auctioned.

The next proprietor, Edward Link, changed the emphasis away from medicine by calling his acquisition the Royal Hotel, Beulah Spa. He did not last long, but the name persisted through the decade. The next owner was Thomas Philip Austin, who sometimes ran the hotel himself, but usually employed managers, Mr and Mrs Palmer in 1865, Thomas Harper in 1867, Richard and Mrs Green in 1869. Such a turnover suggests lack of success, and by 1871 Thomas Sowter, 'independent minister and hydropathic practitioner', was the new master of the Hydropathic Establishment (late Royal Hotel), as the directories called it. Here at last some stability was achieved, for Sowter remained until 1886, and then handed over a going concern to Cephas Barker, who ran the Beulah Spa Hydro and Residential Hotel until the First World War. It was

Barker who demolished Spa Cottage to the west (first acquired by James Fielding in 1842) and replaced it with an ugly ball and concert room.

Barker held the hotel on a repairing lease due to expire in 1928, at a rent of £525 per annum. The freehold had been auctioned in 1913, at which point the advertisements were already highlighting the 'grounds of six acres having prospective building values'. The last landlord was Arthur Monk, who was at the Beulah Spa from 1925 until it closed in 1937. In May of that year it was sold with vacant possession as an 'excellent building estate', and demolished soon after. Most of the five acres of garden that remained were indeed built over, but part at least of the site of the hotel was used for the enlarged Beulah Spa pub.

The Beulah Spa Tap, No.41 Beulah Hill

There was probably a tap attached to the Beulah Spa Hotel from its opening in 1831, or very soon afterwards. The social segregation of the time clearly demanded a separate place of refreshment for the visitors' servants, and the coachmen who ferried them to and from London. It had certainly been established by 1841, when Thomas Figgin was the landlord. But the tap was not then in its familiar position at the corner of Spa Hill. The original location was on the other, western, side of the hotel, conveniently close to the stables where its best customers spent much of their time. This connection was made clear by an advertisement that appeared in 1848: 'wanted, a man & his wife, without encumbrances, to take the management of tap and stables, apply at the Beulah Spa Hotel.' Clearly the tap was sometimes managed by a servant for the benefit of the hotel, but more often it was let to a publican. The standard rent, current in 1861 and 1900, was £100 per annum.

The stables and tap were rebuilt on the Spa Hill corner when the hotel was extended to the west in the late 1850s. Mrs Dee says that 'the Beulah Spa Tap was finished and opened by Mr Preddy'. This was William Preddy, later of the Conquering Hero, who was the tenant for three or four years from 1860 or 1861. He was already established at the Beulah-spa livery stables by October 1859. When there was an intention to sell the hotel in 1861 the particulars stated that:

> On the east side is a valuable Tap, containing three rooms, bar, parlour, tap room, kitchen, etc.; and in the rear, approached under an archway, is a yard and stabling for ten horses, carriage shed, enclosed coach-house, loft, harness room, etc.

This archway is seen in the photograph of the pub on p.21.

The Tap was run by women as often as by men. There was Mrs Fanny Day from 1865-70 (as manager for the proprietor of the hotel), Mrs Elizabeth Butt from 1876-1892, and Mrs A. Fremaut from 1908-1913. Among the men the most notable, on account of his wonderfully appropriate name, was Harry Northwood, who was landlord from 1914-26. A full licence had been obtained by 1913, when the freehold was auctioned. The tenant was then paying £140 per annum. The last licensee was John Hart, who arrived in the mid-1930s and was retained by Charrington's as landlord of the new pub. The hotel was sold in 1937 and probably demolished in that year. The Tap was not included in that sale and was perhaps spared until early in 1939, as Hart continues to be listed as a voter there in every year up to the war. The Tap's replacement is described above as The Beulah Spa.

The former Birkbeck Tavern in 1997.

THE BIRKBECK TAVERN, BIRKBECK HILL

The Birkbeck triangle, squeezed between the railway line, Thurlow Park Road, and Lovelace Road, was a development of the late 1850s, but most of the houses were built in the 1860s and 1870s. The three roads were Birkbeck Street (now Thurlow Hill), Birkbeck Place and Birkbeck Road (now Birkbeck Hill). The surrounding area was predominantly given over to large detached houses, so this was presumably intended, like Norwood New Town off Central Hill, to invisibly accommodate the many service workers required in any prosperous suburb.

Such enclaves tended to be self-sufficient as far as eating and drinking were concerned, and here the shops and the pub were located together on the north side of Birkbeck Place. The Birkbeck Tavern at the corner had two numbers in its earlier days, No.1 Birkbeck Place and No.8 Birkbeck Road. It had been established by 1868, when John Gale was the landlord. In the twentieth century it was run by the Defries family. Harry Defries took it over in 1905, and remained until his death in the mid-1920s. He was succeeded briefly by his widow, Annie Rebecca, and from 1927 by his daughter Miss Lilly Defries, whose name always appears with the double 'l' in directories. She ran the pub until her death around 1956. Her executors were the last holders of the licence. The pub closed in 1959 and was converted into housing.

THE BREWERY TAP, NORWOOD BREWERY, NO.33 CHAPEL ROAD

The Norwood Brewery on the north side of Chapel Road existed by 1851, when John Lewis Lane was the proprietor. He was bankrupt three years later. His main asset was then the remaining seventy-four-year lease of a 'newly erected brick-built and slated brewery, with tap and residence attached'. But although there is this proof that the Tap existed, it is not mentioned in any other sources I have seen until 1880. So it would appear that if the next two brewers, Richard Bennett and George Wadley & Sons, kept the Tap open, they ran it themselves. It was only when Duberly & Brooke took over as brewers in 1880 that the first independent landlord of the Tap appeared, presumably as their tenant. He was James Keniston, who quickly went on to greater things at the Hope. Two other landlords, James Carr in 1884 and John Nurden in 1892, made fleeting appearances before the James family came on the scene in 1895 or 1896. The brewery and its beerhouse struggled on together until brewing came to an end in 1922. The Tap managed to survive independently for a few more years, run by George James until 1924 and William George James until 1927, but it had closed by 1929. The fact that the larger Bricklayers' Arms was only a few yards away cannot have helped. The brewery buildings have been incorporated into the Winn & Coates factory, the office of which has replaced the Tap.

THE BRICKLAYER'S ARMS, NO.29 CHAPEL ROAD

The Bricklayer's Arms was founded in the early 1840s, in an existing semi-detached cottage, by the bricklayer Thomas Wallis, who continued to run it until his death around 1891. He was sometimes described as a bricklayer & beer retailer, sometimes as a builder & beer retailer, so when the original cottage was replaced by something more substantial, which it had been by 1870, it is very likely that Wallis did the job himself. Some builders found it useful to own a pub, as a way of clawing back part of their men's wages.

The second Bricklayer's Arms, Chapel Road, in 1995.

The Bricklayer's Arms, Hamilton Road, in 1995.

Wilson says, 'on Sunday mornings the Bricklayer's Arms was the meeting place of local cyclists with their penny-farthing bicycles. They used to hold a competition to see who could ride from the Bricklayer's Arms to the Gipsy House without getting off.' Wallis set the trend of long service behind the bar at the Bricklayer's Arms. His successors have included Thomas Roberts Watts for more than a decade from 1898, John Thomas Whetter from 1911-31, and William Henry Barnes and other members of the family for more than twenty-five years from 1932. The Bricklayer's Arms has been closed and boarded-up for several years, and its future looks bleak.

THE BRICKLAYER'S ARMS, NO.1 HAMILTON ROAD

The Bricklayer's Arms was built between 1860-67, as part of the development of what is now Carnac Street, but which was then counted as part of Hamilton Road. John Kellaway is the first known licensee. The analogy of the other pub of the name would suggest that he was a builder before becoming a publican, but I have no evidence that it was so. He was here from 1867 or a little earlier until the late 1880s. The Bricklayer's Arms is remarkable in having had only five landlords (that I can trace) in its first ninety years. Kellaway's successors were Robert George Edwards in the early 1890s, Henry James Morgan from 1894-1927, Daniel Alfred Smith from 1929-31, and Harry Robert Jolley from 1932-58 or later. Such a record suggests prosperity and contentment, and the pub continues to serve its district, in the handsome original building, even in the difficult conditions of today.

The Brunswick, No.1 Anerley Road

The Brunswick, which was sometimes known as the Brunswick Inn or Hotel, stood at the south-eastern corner of Anerley Road (or Hill) and Crystal Palace Station Road. Its original address was No.6 Brunswick Parade, the name for the shops that began next to the station and ended at Brunswick Place. It became No.1 Anerley Road in the early 1880s. The pub was the creation (in 1862) of Charles Pawley of Sydenham, 'an extensive builder', who tried to obtain a licence in the following year. His barrister alleged 'the preference shown by the railway officials generally for his client's house, which was the nearest to the station, together with the large amount of business done there weekly, although no spirits had been sold.' But Pawley was frustrated by the opposition of James Careless of the Paxton Arms. When the magistrates granted a licence to William Blake Stannard in March 1864 they did so on the grounds that a new pub would be 'a great accommodation to workmen in the neighbourhood'. That would seem to suggest that the existing establishments in Anerley Hill, the Rising Sun, the Paxton Arms, and the Star Hotel were not welcoming to workmen, which is surprising in the case of the Rising Sun. The last landlord, Frederick John Dawson, is honorably mentioned in *Signs of the Times*:

> With Dawson comfortably seated
> In good old 'Brunswick's Arms'.

A sixty-three-year remainder lease of the Brunswick Hotel, Anerley Hill, was sold for £305 in 1920. The purchaser was apparently not a publican, for very soon the building had become the British Steam Dye Works, which did cleaning as well as dyeing. The area was heavily bombed during the Second World War, and the site of the wrecked Brunswick is now the open space in front of the block of flats known as Brunswick Court.

The California Hotel and Tea Garden, Gipsy Hill

Tea gardens were all the rage in Norwood from the 1830s until the middle of the 1850s, when that apotheosis of the tea garden, the Crystal Palace, eclipsed them all. Fine views were one of the ingredients required by these establishments, and there are few more dramatic in Norwood than the ones from Gipsy Hill. In the early days after the enclosure of the common this was a sparsely occupied area, used mainly for brick making. The land that is now on the north or downhill side of Highland Road held only two small cottages. By 1850 one was occupied by a supplier of loam called William Sparshott. The other he had probably turned into a house of entertainment, as he is listed in 1851 as the proprietor of tea gardens. Three years later, no doubt in fear of the imminent competition of the Crystal Palace, he or his landlord was offering for sale, 'a lease at £100 per annum of the well-known California Hotel and Tea Gardens, situate on Gipsy-hill, with one-and-a-half acres of ground, on which with a judicious outlay of a small sum of money very extensive stabling might be erected'. This is almost the last we hear of the California, and it is doubtful whether the judicious outlay was ever made.

Recalling his youth in 1907 the old Norwood resident Edward Wheeler wrote that 'at the corner of Highland Road, where The Highlands now stands, was the old California Tea Gardens, where tea and anything else they pleased could be had', which strongly suggests that alcohol was also available. By 1864 certainly, and probably by 1861, the tea gardens had been replaced by the house known at first as Highlands, and later as Heraklea or Saxawald, which was demolished in

The Cambridge Hotel, *c.*1914.

the mid-1930s. Part of the site is now occupied by Highlands Court. The tea gardens extended to Gipsy Hill, as did originally the garden of the house.

THE CAMBRIDGE, NO.2 CHURCH ROAD AND/OR 90 WESTOW HILL

Once the Crystal Palace came to Norwood the three corner sites facing it at the Triangle became highly valuable for hotels and pubs. One was already occupied by the White Swan, and the second was immediately taken for the Royal Crystal Palace Hotel. The third, at the corner of Church Road and Westow Hill, did not become available until after 1857, when Aubin's Central London poor law school was removed. The Cambridge was probably built there in 1861, as it was open by February 1862. In March of that year:

> Mr Henry Salmon Gifford, proprietor of the Cambridge Restaurant, Hotel, etc., Norwood, applied for a spirit licence. Mr W. Drummond described the hotel as being conducted on the continental principle, and it was intended to combine the advantages of an hotel, a lodging-house, and a boarding-house. Mr Drummond produced a number of testimonials from noblemen and gentlemen, and commented on the great want of hotel accommodation in the neighbourhood of the Crystal Palace. Mr Childs opposed on behalf of the White Swan, the Crystal Palace Hotel Company, and other inns in the vicinity. It having transpired that Mr Gifford had not yet signed the lease, the Bench adjourned, intimating that the licence would be granted on production of the lease, duly signed.

As it was licenced as an hotel, and was advertised as the Cambridge Family Hotel in 1863, there was considerable opposition from the neighbouring landlords two years later when there was an attempt to transform it into an ordinary pub. The magistrates approved of the Cambridge, however, 'not only on the grounds of the large accommodation the bar afforded, but also in consideration that there would be a large increase of traffic when the railway operations were completed.' The process of evolution into a mere pub was apparently delayed, as the style of the house during the rest of the 1860s was the Cambridge Hotel and Restaurant, but by the 1870s it was usually known as the Cambridge Tavern. Notable landlords have been the splendidly named Zachariah John Selth from 1877-84, and Jack Flatau, 'with his winged collar and tailed suit', who died in office in October 1955, after twenty-one years as licensee. The pub's commanding position gives it a deceptively spacious appearance, but it is built on a restricted plot in the sharp angle of Church Road and Westow Hill, so that the bar is surprisingly small.

THE CAMBRIDGE CASTLE, SOUTH NORWOOD HIGH STREET

This is little more than a name. Early in 1867 William Few was refused a licence for the Cambridge Castle, South Norwood High Street. The fact that the house already had a sign might suggest that it had opened as a beer shop, but I can find no trace of it before or after, and cannot say where in the High Street it stood.

THE CANTERBURY ARMS, LANSDOWNE HILL

This was another obscure and short-lived pub. It probably stood at the corner of Canterbury Grove. Thomas Dillon was listed as a beer retailer at 'Sydenham terrace, Lansdowne Hill' in an 1870 directory. In the 1871 census Thomas Dillon, beerhouse keeper, appears at the Canterbury Arms in Lansdowne Hill. The pub makes no earlier or later appearances in the records, or none that I have found.

THE CASTLE, NO.21 NORWOOD HIGH STREET

This pub has had a circular history. It was built in the 1860s as a detached corner shop, being used by a grocer in 1872. During the next few years other shops were built alongside and the grocery was converted into a beerhouse as the Castle. The first licensee was probably Mrs Emily McBurney, who was here in 1876. I can only name three other licensees. William Hill was probably at the Castle in 1878. He is the only beer retailer in the High Street at that time not otherwise accounted for. George Jeater (formerly a baker in Hamilton Road) certainly was the landlord from 1880-84, and Richard Thorn from 1886-1894. By 1896 Arthur Pedder had turned the pub into dining rooms, a use that continued at least until the 1950s. But now the old pub, once again deprived of its neighbours by demolition, has returned to its original function as a grocer's shop. In 2006 a huge rear extension was added, doubling the size of the building.

Standing at the entrance to one of West Norwood's slums the Castle was naturally not for the genteel. According to J.B. Wilson, 'the local name for this public house was the Roaring Donkey because of the fights that took place there, especially on Saturday nights'.

The former Castle, *c.*1934. (Lambeth Archives)

THE CLARENDON HOTEL, NO.47 BEULAH HILL

This building just west of the Beulah Spa Hotel began and ended its career as a private house, but for a few years in the 1850s it was caught up in the Crystal Palace boom that led to the founding of so many hotels and pubs in Norwood. It was built in 1851 by James Franks, a notable local developer who was also responsible for the Queen's Hotel, and was first occupied by the northern mining magnate, Sir George Denys, who called his new home Mizpah. Sir George only remained in Norwood until 1855.

With his departure Franks seized the opportunity to increase his share of the profits expected from entertaining visitors to the Crystal Palace. In April 1856 his new venture was announced, with the usual journalistic accuracy, in *The Times*:

> Queen's and the Clarendon Hotels: Clarendon Hotel, Upper Norwood, near the Beulah-spa gardens, in connection with the Queen's Hotel. – The nobility, clergy, and gentry are specially informed that the delightfully situate mansion, recently the residence of Sir George Denny, Bart., is now open for the reception of visitors, by the name of the Clarendon Hotel, under the same management as the Queen's Hotel.

It was presumably named after the fourth Earl of Clarendon, then Foreign Secretary.

Left: The former Clarendon Hotel, *c.*1910.

Opposite: The Clifton Arms in 1908. (John Gent)

The Clarendon was promoted as a more retired and select alternative for those who found the Queen's too large and bustling. It was also, no doubt, intended to damage the business of the nearly adjoining Beulah Spa Hotel, one of the Queen's most serious rivals, which was then closed for rebuilding. Whatever the motive behind Franks's scheme, it was not a success. The Crystal Palace did not attract so many resident visitors as local optimists had hoped, and several of the hastily opened hotels closed with almost equal haste. The Clarendon lasted only until 1859, when the Beulah Spa Hotel reopened. Its failure was not held against the resident manager, Thomas Holt, who moved to the senior position of managing the Queen's itself. The Clarendon reverted to its original role as a private residence, now known as Clarendon House. It was divided into flats in the late 1920s, and demolished in the 1950s. A block of flats now occupies the site, on the eastern corner of Spurgeon Road.

THE CLIFTON ARMS, NO.21 CLIFTON ROAD

The Clifton Arms, a stately three-storeyed pub on a corner site, was opened as a beerhouse, probably in 1865. Two men, John Lascelles and Henry Bailey, applied unsuccessfully for a full licence in 1865 and 1866 before Jehu Joy Hunt obtained one in 1867. He did not enjoy this triumph for long, as he died early in 1869 and his widow a few days after him. The executors transferred the licence to Thomas Hart. As some indication of what the area was like at that time, James Richard Greening, the licensee in the early 1870s, is listed in the census as a 'publican and farmer'.

The most notable of the early landlords was George William Amer, who was at the Clifton Arms from 1878-84, before beginning a long reign at the South Norwood Railway Hotel, now the Cherry Tree. Other long-serving publicans were William Robert Coleman for more than a decade either side of 1900, and the lady who under the successive names of Mrs Pullen and Mrs Collison was in charge from the early 1920s until the mid-1950s. It was in her time that the volume and nature of the trade must have changed substantially with the establishment of the Crystal Palace FC ground on the opposite corner of Holmesdale Road. More recently this pub adjoining Selhurst Park has surprisingly been run by Dave Harper, a former Millwall footballer, and father of the actor Frank Harper. Architects will not be surprised to hear that the skimpy pediments above the two main sides of the building are modern additions.

THE COACH & HORSES, GIPSY ROAD

William Benton, a grocer and small-scale property developer, has left a permanent mark in West Norwood by giving his name to Benton's Lane. Throughout the 1850s the third string to his bow was a beer shop known grandiosely as the Coach & Horses, a name usually associated with large posting inns. The address of this pub is given in directories and advertisements either as Elder Road, which was then sometimes used for the central section of Gipsy Road, or as Mount Pleasant, which was the area bounded in modern terms by Gipsy Road, St Gothard Road, the southern wall of the cemetery, Hubbard Road and Auckland Road. It seems clear from the 1851 census that the Coach & Horses was on the north side of Gipsy Road, but I have not been able to determine exactly where. In 1845 Timothy Pressley had a beer shop – replaced before 1870 by two semi-detached houses – on the eastern corner of Gipsy Road and St Gothard Road. This may have been the same establishment, but the 1851 census seems to place the Coach & Horses rather more to the west.

The last record of Benton as a publican comes from an 1860 directory, where he is described as a, 'grocer and beer retailer, Gipsy Hill'. A number of buildings in Gipsy Road were destroyed when the railway cutting was dug in 1856. Possibly the Coach & Horses was one of the casualties, forcing Benton to move his business elsewhere. But given the frequent inaccuracy of directories, and the fact that Benton is otherwise associated entirely with the Gipsy Road area, it is more likely that the 1860 entry is mistaken and that Benton was still at the Coach & Horses. (It is perhaps significant that this same 1860 directory places the Gipsy Tavern in Gipsy Hill.) The 1861 census shows Benton as a grocer at No.2 Roberts Place, which was on the south side of Gipsy Road, near Benton's Lane. I have found no later reference to the Coach & Horses.

The Colby Arms in 2006.

THE COLBY ARMS, NO.132 GIPSY HILL

This was part of the development of Colby Road, which was begun in 1867. The building has entrances in Gipsy Hill and Colby Road. The full original name of the pub, the Colby Arms Railway Tavern, indicates sufficiently the reason for establishing a pub here. Gipsy Hill station had been opened in 1856. The building existed by 1870, but is first recorded as a pub in the 1871 census, where James Sanderson is listed at the Colby Arms as a wine merchant. In a directory of 1872 he is given as a beer retailer. Sanderson was to remain the publican until 1886, by which time he was seventy-five. His long-serving successors were George White for more than a decade either side of 1900, Henry M. Forsey during the 1920s, and Charles H. Harward from 1940-52, latterly in partnership with William Bell. In the mid- 1960s Dick Mills was landlord before migrating to the White Swan. The Colby Arms is a fine looking pub, despite the loss, some time since the Second World War, of the dignified porch that used to grace the Gipsy Hill entrance.

THE CONQUERING HERO, NO.262 BEULAH HILL

When George Hunt applied for a licence for the Conquering Hero in 1865 he told the magistrates that he had spent £2,000 on improving the building, which was his freehold, and on providing stables. He also reminded them that he had run the Beulah Retreat for five years without any complaint. The magistrates were impressed and took the uncommon step of granting a licence immediately. What Hunt did not tell them was the meaning of the name he had chosen for his pub. Then it was no doubt obvious from the sign, but now the identity of the hero is a mystery. Rupert Montagu Browne, an old Beulah Hill resident, writing in 1917,

The Conquering Hero, *c.* 1909, with
a possible hero inset.

claimed that the Conquering Hero 'owed its title to the victory won by mine host over the
neighbouring gentry - Mr Salmon, Mr Flight, and others - who protested against a beerhouse
so near their properties'. Other writers have suggested that the hero was Garibaldi, who visited
Norwood Grove in 1864. In support of this theory is the fact that when Garibaldi went to the
Crystal Palace in May of that year the band greeted him with Handel's *See the Conquering Hero
Comes*. A Victorian postcard of the pub features an inset portrait of a Crimean cavalry officer,
presumably copied from one displayed inside, seeming to imply that this was the hero.

If George Hunt was the conqueror of his snobbish neighbours, he was himself soon
vanquished by a ghost from his past. When Hunt was at the Beulah Retreat his nearest rival
was William Preddy of the Beulah Spa Tap. Hunt had hardly finished celebrating his triumph in
obtaining a licence at the Conquering Hero when one Henry Charles Preddy arrived on the
scene to build the Fountain Head beerhouse

next door to him. He ran it for a year, then handed over to William Preddy. The sole purpose of this
short-lived parasitical establishment appears to have been the harassment of poor George Hunt.
He was already in trouble with the authorities because of the fouling of the Crown Pond

The remains of the former Crown in 2006.

(adjoining the pub in Beulah Hill) by seepage from the urinals and cellar of the Conquering Hero. The horses would perhaps not have complained had it been only the cellars. The disturbance to the ground level caused by the building of the Fountain Head added to the problems by flooding Hunt's pub with rain water. By 1871 he was defeated. His victorious rival took over the Conquering Hero and closed the beerhouse.

The most prominent of the later landlords have been Harry R. Russell from 1896-1906, Alfred Izatt from 1916-26, and various members of the King family throughout the 1930s. The Conquering Hero is kept in good decorative condition, and with its prominent location and attendant pond is one of the most picturesque of the Norwood pubs.

THE CROWN, NO.129 HAMILTON ROAD

This was a small and obscure beerhouse known to the locals, according to Wilson, as the Bug & Bolster, presumably in jocular criticism of the sign. It stood on the outer angle of the bend in Hamilton Road, just east of Clive Road, and very close to the Hamilton Arms. Hamilton Road was 'new' in 1852, so it is possible that the house that became The Crown was built not long after that, but its first probable appearance as a pub is in 1868, when George Ward is listed as a beer retailer in Hamilton Road. There was a builder of that name in Chancellor Road (now Chancellor Grove) in 1871. Given the close relationship between the two trades, he may well have been the same man. The Crown certainly existed by 1872, by which time John Grove had begun a fifteen-year stint as landlord. Much his longest-serving successor was John Newton, who was in charge from 1908 until the end of the Second World War. The pub remained in the family, being run by Percy George Newton until at least 1958. The Crown was closed in the late 1970s. The present No.129 appears to be the old pub rather drastically converted into a private house.

THE CROWN & ANCHOR, WESTOW HILL

In an advertisement published in 1835 this establishment 'near the Woodman inn at Norwood' was described as:

> The Crown & Anchor beer shop and tea gardens, affording excellent accommodation for company, with coach houses, stabling, and other appendages. The property stands on the summit of Westow-Hill, and commands a most delightful and extensive view of the rich scenery of the surrounding country, including the river Thames and the metropolis, and is most attractive in the summer season. The premises are let to a most respectable tenant, who has expended several hundred pounds in enlarging and improving the property.

(In advertisements, though not alas in life, all tenants are respectable.)
There were several unlocated beer sellers in Westow Hill at the time, but nothing more is heard of one using this sign. The view of the Thames and metropolis suggests the Lambeth side of Westow Hill, but, 'near the Woodman' may mean that this was the forerunner of the Royal Albert.

THE DAGMAR ARMS, NOS 257 AND 259 ROMMANY ROAD

Dagmar Road was the original name, in the 1870s, for what was later the northern end of Rommany Road. Post-war changes, with the construction of a council estate to replace many of the old houses and the pedestrianisation of part of the area, have made the topography hard to grasp, especially as the site of the pub is now counted as part of St Gothard Road. It was nearly opposite the western end of Hamilton Grove (itself now extinguished) and separated from the cemetery only by a narrow strip of land belonging to the pottery.

There is a puzzle connected with its earliest years. George Liversuch was the first landlord, and by 1882 he was certainly established at what was later Nos 257 and 259 Rommany Road. But he is listed as a beer retailer in Dagmar Road in an 1870 directory, at a time when the OS map shows buildings only on the east side of the new road, at the northern end opposite the pottery. Unless the southern end of Dagmar Road was developed very quickly in 1870, this may suggest that Liversuch began in one of these original houses, then moved his establishment to a new and larger building as the road was extended during the 1870s. George Liversuch remained in charge until 1886, after which there were only two more landlords, George Robert Kellaway and Frederick Brown, before the Dagmar Arms closed in 1900. The building, which was no doubt originally designed as two units, reverted to type, No.257 becoming a private dwelling and No.259 a greengrocer's shop. Both were demolished in 1969, when the council yard behind was enlarged.

THE DUKE OF CLARENCE, NO.57 PORTLAND ROAD

This small, attractive, unpretentious pub was a beerhouse from its foundation around 1866 until such invidious class distinctions were swept away. The first landlord was Alfred Holder who, fresh from his failure to get a full licence for the Alliance, was equally unsuccessful here in 1868 and 1869. At the following year's licensing session the new landlord, William Cooper, employed

The Duke of Clarence in 1999; the bunting was outside the Queen's Arms opposite.

an advocate to represent him, whose eloquence deserved a more distinguished stage. He argued that the Duke of Clarence deserved a licence because it was now a Foresters' Court with an excellent club room. An even more compelling reason was that there were 'such frequent applications for spirits that it made both the landlord and his wife quite miserable to have to deny them'. Licence refused. The longest-serving landlord of the Clarence was William Herbert Vousley, who was there from the late 1890s to the early 1930s. The Clarence is still going strong, having apparently seen off its older and larger rival, the Queen's Arms, which stood nearly opposite.

THE DUKE OF CORNWALL, NO.41 CAWNPORE STREET OR 41 WOODLAND ROAD

This little beerhouse stood at the corner of Cawnpore (formerly George) Street and Woodland Road, a position that coincidentally gave it the number 41 in both. As it had doors in each street nobody could decide to which it properly belonged, so sometimes it was listed in one, sometimes in the other. Cawnpore Street was, I think, its true home, as there is some reason to believe that before the street numbering was established it began as part of Palace Villas, George Street, the address at which George Plant, beer retailer, is listed in 1870. At that time the pub was the only part of this group of houses that had been completed, but when the dust settled the Duke of Cornwall found itself at No.13 Palace Villas. That might have encouraged a superstitious landlord to emphasise the Woodland Road connection. The longest-serving landlord was Edward James

The former Duke of Edinburgh in 2003.

Noakes, who arrived at the beginning of the First World War and stayed until 1927. The last was William Hardie. The pub, which was too close to the larger Railway Bell for prosperity, closed in 1935. The building served as a laundry for the few years until it was destroyed in the Second World War.

THE DUKE OF EDINBURGH, NO.23 WESTOW STREET

The Duke of Edinburgh was Queen Victoria's second son Alfred, who was given his dukedom in 1866 as some compensation for having to decline the crown of Greece. The Norwood pub named after him was another notably unsuccessful one, which lasted for less than twenty years. It is first heard of in December 1867, when 'Frankenburgh' was rated for a beerhouse in Westow Street. There had been a baker's shop on the site earlier in the 1860s, but the architectural style suggests that that and its neighbour (No.21) had just been rebuilt. In January 1868 a local paper tells us that the Croydon Board of Health had received a letter from Mr Frankenburgh, landlord of the Duke of Edinburgh Inn, Norwood, reporting that he had removed the roof of his skittle-alley, as ordered. Skittles was a popular Victorian pub game, also played at the Ship. This covered alley in the garden apparently struck the official mind as being inadequately ventilated.

Later in 1868 Henry Constable, better known as Harry, who had previously been in business as a corn merchant on the opposite side of Westow Street, is listed at the Duke of Edinburgh beer shop. Very soon he was in trouble with the police, and fined for opening his pub out of hours. That was perhaps why an ex-policeman, George Seaward Beltham (or Beldon or Baldham – the reports vary) was put up to apply for a full licence. In 1871 he argued that the working men of the district, intimidated by the splendour of the White Hart and the Holly Bush, needed a place of their own, but the magistrates were not convinced. The Edinburgh struggled on as a beer shop, run by Constable and others, until 1884, when Mrs C. King was the proprietor. It was then empty for a number of years – an 1889 directory described it as an unoccupied beerhouse – before being converted into a shop. Mrs Jane Hurst was installed there as a greengrocer by 1892. The old pub is now a clothes shop.

THE EAGLE TAVERN, NO.26 DOVER ROAD

The address of this pub was very fluid. Sources place it in Albert Road, New Town, at No.1 Truscott Terrace, and in various other places before the final Dover Road harbour was reached. Among the pubs of Norwood New Town the Eagle occupied an intermediate role between the short-lived Fox under the Hill and the enduring Oxford Arms. The Eagle's distinction was to have been the first pub founded in this working class enclave south of Central Hill. It certainly existed by 1855, when 'Joseph Chamberlain, beer retailer, Central Hill, Norwood New Town' was listed in a directory. In the 1855 rate book his address is given as Central Valley. Chamberlain was the owner of the pub. The fact that he did not remain the publican for long might suggest that he was also the builder.

Robert Vale was granted a full licence 'for a house at Truscott Terrace, New Town' in 1856. Isaac Smith, the licensee by 1859, had previously been at the Beulah Retreat. He remained at the Eagle long enough to make neighbourly objection to the Oxford's applications for a licence in 1864 and 1865, perhaps retiring in disgust when one was granted. He had originally moved to the Eagle from the Beulah Retreat to escape competition from the Beulah Spa Tap. None of his successors at the Eagle stayed for long. The last was Thomas Harris, who was in charge in 1890. By 1892 the Eagle had closed its doors. The building was never used as a pub again. Beryl Cheeseman says it was demolished around 1911 after a Mr and Mrs Rednapp had lived there as caretakers for a number of years. But maps seem to show the old Eagle surviving until at least 1933, with new buildings not indicated on the site until after the Second World War.

THE FORESTER'S ARMS, NO.90 NORWOOD HIGH STREET

The Forester's Arms was a small, obscure and short-lived beerhouse, entirely overshadowed by its eminent neighbour, the King's Head. It was founded in the mid-1860s by John Cooper. Wilson says that 'the landlord of this public house would not allow women to enter it, and there was a spinning jenny on the ceiling which was a popular way of deciding who should pay for the drinks.' The career of the Forester's Arms ended, like so much else, in 1914. The last landlord was Frank Newton, who moved to the Hope. The building was converted into a shop. Now, greatly altered, it is an office.

THE FOUNTAIN HEAD, NOS 264 AND 266 BEULAH HILL

This beerhouse had one of the shortest and much the oddest history of any Norwood pub. It appears to have been founded purely to annoy the landlord of the Conquering Hero next door

The Forester's Arms around 1908, Frank Newton with the binoculars. (Lambeth Archives)

(Crown & Anchor), and was closed as soon as it had fulfilled its purpose by driving him away. The Preddy family, which provided the only two landlords, was long-established in Norwood. Joseph Preddy, who was probably the first licensee of the White Swan, ran several shops in Crown Lane from the 1840s until 1880, as corn & coal merchant, grocer, draper, and provision dealer. William Preddy was landlord of the Beulah Spa Tap, and as such a neighbour and rival of George Hunt of the Conquering Hero, when he was at the Beulah Retreat.

In 1867 or 1868, two or three years after Hunt's triumphant move to the Conquering Hero, Henry Charles Preddy set up as a beer seller at the newly built Fountain Head next door. Within a year he handed over the beer shop to William Preddy, while retaining part of the premises for use as a dairy. William was soon involved in disputes with George Hunt about flooding. After three years of living next to Preddy, Hunt had had enough. Late in 1871 or early in 1872 he left the Conquering Hero, on which he had spent £2,000, and William Preddy triumphantly took his place. The Fountain Head was immediately closed, after a mere five years. Rate books continue to list it as an unoccupied beerhouse until 1878 or 1879, but there is good evidence that it was turned to other uses. In 1872 it is listed as a grocer's shop occupied by Joseph Predley, which is very likely a misprint for Preddy. From 1876 part of the old beerhouse was occupied by Frederick William Garnham, a builder, and it was probably he who added the shop fronts and chose the dignified new name, Beulah Place, that can still be seen displayed on the front wall of Nos 264 and 266 Beulah Hill.

THE FOX AND HOUNDS, No.19 EAST PLACE

This little beerhouse was hidden away in an obscure side street behind the Hope, and overshadowed by the railway viaduct running into West Norwood station. It was probably founded around 1870 by Thomas Relph, who was there in 1871, and described as a carpenter and beer seller. Tradesmen ambitious of founding a small pub often began in this tentative fashion. By 1878 he was just a beer retailer. The building existed in 1870, but the large room at the back (mentioned below) had not then been added, so probably it was still a cottage just like its neighbours. Of Relph's few successors the only one who stayed for long was the last landlord, Michael T. Exeter, who was there for a decade.

Wilson says that it:

> was always referred to locally as the Old Top Hat because someone had once climbed to the top of its swinging signpost and placed a top hat on it. This hat remained there for so long that it gave the public house its nickname. Behind the Fox & Hounds was a large room where the local bird fanciers would gather on a Sunday morning. I have seen an old handbill advertising 'A Smoking Concert to be held at the Fox & Hounds, East Place, for the benefit of Mr ..., who, owing to the death of his wife, has been left entirely without support'.

The Fox & Hounds closed in 1910, an early sacrifice to the Licensing Act of 1904, which encouraged magistrates to get rid of superfluous pubs. The building was taken over by a firewood dealer: an appeal, in this impoverished area, to an even more basic human need than alcohol. The former pub was demolished in 1937-38, together with the rest of East Place, as part of a slum clearance drive.

Opposite: The former Fountain Head in 1997.

Right: The Fox & Hounds seen from the railway viaduct in the 1870s. (Upper Norwood Joint Library)

THE FOX UNDER THE HILL, NO.36 EAGLE HILL

The shortest-lived of the three Norwood New Town pubs was the Fox under the Hill beerhouse. It closed before the naming or numbering of its road was fixed, so the exact location is not quite certain. It was in Eagle Hill, formerly known as Spa Road or Spa New Road, and probably on the west side of the southern section sometimes called Little Eagle Hill, about a third of the way between the kink and Chevening Road. The Fox had only one landlord, a former policeman named William Marsh, who persevered with the venture from 1869 until 1884. In a poor district, and with the not notably prosperous Eagle nearby, the pickings must have been lean. If I have correctly identified the building, it survived as a private house numbered No.36 Eagle Hill until the almost total clearance of New Town in the 1960s.

THE FREEMASON'S TAVERN, NO.81 PENGE ROAD

The Freemason's Tavern was built by Abraham Steer, the man responsible for developing the area of luxurious housing known as South Norwood Park, on the other side of the railway line. At the time of his connection with the pub, Steer was living close by at the South Norwood Park lodge, now No.11 Lancaster Road. The naming, if not the building, of the pub was presumably connected with the foundation of the South Norwood Lodge of Freemasons in the winter of 1866-67. It certainly existed as a beerhouse by early 1868, when Steer applied for a full licence. He obtained one in 1869, and promptly transferred it to the first of a long line of full-time publicans, while he returned to his building work across the tracks. The most enduring of the landlords was T.E. Sedge, who was at the Freemason's for much of the first half of the twentieth

The Freemason's Tavern in 1960. (Croydon Local Studies Library)

century. Penge Road has been particularly hard hit by the great shake-out of pubs that began in 1989, when the brewers were forced to shed many of their tied houses. The Freemason's Tavern closed in 2002, and the building has now been converted into flats.

THE GEORGE IV (1), GIPSY HILL

The original George IV, one of the leading inns of Norwood, was certainly founded by 1829, and may have existed as early as 1824. I have not seen the name in use before 1832, but there can be little doubt of its going back to the foundation. King George was unpopular enough while on the throne to make the naming of a pub after him rather uncommon. After his death it is unimaginable. (J.B. Wilson makes the claim, for which I can find no support, that 'Gypsy Hill was originally called King William IV Hill after a little public house which stood close by the corner of Woodland Road'.) A man named Hunt may have been living in the building in 1824, but I have no evidence that he was an innkeeper. Alfred Berry, who certainly was, had taken possession by 1829.

This original George IV inn was on the northern corner of College Street, which is now part of Woodland Road. The green beside Forbes Court occupies the site today. It was a large building with an extensive range of stabling to the north, and probably with pleasure grounds in the rear. Alfred Berry ran it until the 1840s, and was succeeded by William Matthews. Matthews is still listed there in 1855, and on Boxing Day 1856 there was a fight in the George IV public

The former George IV (2) in 1997.

house on 'Gipsy-hill' that landed the aggressor in court, but after that I can find no references to the inn. The site is shown as empty on a map surveyed around 1860, and in 1861 a group of six semi-detached houses known as Gipsy Hill Villas (later Nos 90-100) was built there. The inn may have fallen victim to a fire or some other disaster, but a more likely cause of the change is the all too familiar one of redevelopment. The opening of Gipsy Hill station in 1856 had turned this into prime villa country, and the inn had a temptingly large garden.

THE GEORGE IV (2), NO.86 GIPSY HILL

No.86 Gipsy Hill, the car breakers' shop that was demolished in 2000, served as the George IV beerhouse for seven decades. There seems to have been no connection, except the imitative one of the name, between this and the nearby George IV inn. The beerhouse was a two-storey cottage built in 1829, originally detached, but by 1850 incorporated into a terrace. The first occupants were Richard Roles, a wood broker, and his wife Sillister. They were the parents of Thomas Roles, also a wood broker, who was listed there in the 1841 census. It is curious that he appeared in 1839 as a witness at an inquest held at the old George IV.

There is reason to think that the cottage had become a beerhouse even before the closure of the old inn, for in 1851 Sarah Wherrit, a forty-four-year-old beer shop keeper, was either at No.86 or very close by. She can hardly have called her house the George IV while the original inn existed, but what other name she gave it I am unable to say, unless it was Wilson's William IV, or perhaps the Royal Standard. If Sarah Wherrit was running her beer shop at No.86 the use did not last long, for in 1861 Edwin Hurdle, a twenty-four-year-old waiter, was living there with his wife and child and two lodgers. Could he have been a waiter thrown out of work by the closure of the old George IV? It is an unlikely but intriguing possibility, as by 1867 Edwin Hurdle was firmly established as the proprietor, and perhaps the founder, of the new George IV beerhouse at No.86. It is very understandable that he should wish to inherit some fragment of the renown and custom of a now departed neighbour. Perhaps the building of Gipsy Hill Villas in 1861, which extinguished any possibility of reviving the old licence, emboldened Hurdle to appropriate the name.

Thereafter a fairly complete list of publicans can be traced. All were beer retailers, licenced to sell only beer and cider. The longest-serving were John Cox from 1871-86, and George Henry Skillern from 1905-16. His daughter Grace Stymonds contributed some memories to the *Norwood Review* in 2001. She recalled that the pub 'had three bars in the front and a tap room at the back where the customers played darts etc. Dad passed the beers through a window on the door and the drone of the men put my sister and me to sleep of a night.' The George IV was closed in 1935 or 1936, as part of a drive to reduce the number of beerhouses. The building served as the Gipsy Hill Social Club before the war and as a greengrocer's shop afterwards. In 1952 began a long association with motor car spare parts that lasted until the late 1990s. The second George IV was demolished in March 2000, nearly a century and a half after the first, and two houses were soon built on the site.

THE GIPSY HILL HOTEL, NO.79 GIPSY HILL

The opening of Gipsy Hill station in 1856 created an opportunity for a successful hotel in the immediate vicinity. When it was missed or spurned by the original George IV the projectors of the Gipsy Hill Hotel reaped the benefit. There is evidence that the pub was founded in an existing house and not rebuilt in its present form until 1868. An account of the hotel published in 1893 claimed that it 'dates back some thirty years', but that it was rebuilt five or six years after its foundation. The plan with a July 1863 lease of land in Victoria Road shows a large plain rectangular building here belonging to Mr Wenham, perhaps the Henry Wenham who was a grocer in Westow Hill. William Blake Stannard is listed at the Gipsy Hill Hotel in 1867 and 1868, but in July of the latter year there was a sale of the furniture and effects on the premises, which was often a prelude to rebuilding. When the hotel reappeared in the records in 1870 it had a new master, William Gill. An 1870 map shows the hotel irregularly shaped, as it is today.

Percy Robert Bush, one of the longer-serving landlords, had an unhappy beginning and end to his decade in charge. His first year, 1898, was marked by the death of his wife at the age of forty-two. In 1908, his last, he had a fight with Arthur Hill, his manager, and formerly his potman, who was sent to prison for a month for assault. Notable among the later landlords were the Turners (including the magniloquently named Walter Thomas Imperial Turner) from 1926-36, and the Cornells from 1937-53. The Gipsy Hill Hotel, a tall, solid building with a dignified porch, continues to adorn one of Norwood's most graceful roads.

THE GIPSY QUEEN, NO.20 NORWOOD HIGH STREET

This pub has no claim to be called the Gipsy Queen more specific than the general association of Norwood with the tribe. It was founded after the gypsies had vanished from the area, and

The Gipsy Hill Hotel in 1893.

become a piece of picturesque local tradition. The first trace I have discovered of the name is in 1870, when William Booty was the landlord, but it seems likely that James Ballinger was the founder of the Gipsy Queen. He appears as a beer retailer in Gloucester Road (now Cotswold Road) in 1867 and in the High Street in 1868. The pub stands at the corner of those roads, with an entrance in each. Cotswold Road was created in the mid-1860s in belated response to the opening of the station in 1856. The later landlords do not call for much comment, except perhaps the grandly named Laceby Oglesby, there in 1894, and George Hawkins, who presided from 1931 to 1942.

There was a major internal rearrangement in 1969, when the off-sales section that used to divide the public from the saloon bar was removed, and the space gained was used to enlarge the saloon bar. The Gipsy Queen continued to dispense hospitality to commuters, though rather in the shadow both of West Norwood station and the much grander Norwood Hotel until its closure in 2006.

THE GIPSY TAVERN, NO.69 GIPSY ROAD

The Gipsy Tavern is presumably so named merely because it is in Gipsy Road, or Gipsy House Road as it was still called when the pub was founded. The road led to the Old Gipsy House, the wanderers' meeting place that stood in the angle of Gipsy Road and Gipsy Hill. Because the Gipsy Tavern was founded by James Austin as a sideline only it is hard to know precisely when he began to sell beer in addition to his other activities. He was already living in a house on

The Gipsy Queen from the railway bridge in 1998.

or near this site by 1824, but in 1841 he was set down in the census as a labourer. In 1827 *The Times* published a facetious account of a gipsy wedding feast at 'The Old Gipsy House, where they were most sumptuously regaled upon the occasion'. As there is reason to believe that the original Old Gipsy House had been demolished by that time, the 1827 report may well be the first reference to Austin's beerhouse. On the other hand, an account of a carriage accident in 1831 seems to place the Gipsy House at the top of Gipsy Hill. The horse bolted 'down the hill at Norwood leading from the Gipsy-house to Dulwich', and ended up in the front garden of the George IV, about halfway down Gipsy Hill. In 1839 it was stated that the gypsies congregated at the Windmill in Westow Hill.

Describing a walk along Gipsy Road in 1842, Samuel Phillips, writing many years later, recalled that 'at the top of the hill stood the old 'Gipsy-house', dirty & disreputable'. In 1845 a directory lists 'James Austin, beer retailer and grocery dealer, Mount Pleasant', which was a name for the central section of Gipsy Road; and in the 1851 census the entry is for 'Charles Stewart, beer shop keeper, Gypsey House, Gypsey House Road'. The Stewarts were related to the Austins, and the business is called Austin's Beer shop in the description of the census taker's route. Charles Stewart appears in 1852 as a grocer and beer retailer, Elder Road (another name sometimes used for this part of Gipsy Road), in 1855 he was Charles James Stewart, beer retailer, Mount Pleasant, Gipsey Hill, and in 1860 Charles James Stewart, beer retailer, Gipsy Hill. A more modern address was achieved in the 1861 census, where Rebecca Stewart, the widow of Charles, is listed as a beerhouse keeper at Gipsey House, Gipsey Road.

It was apparently the next landlord, James Conway or Conivery, who in the 1860s began to claim a spurious connection with the original gypsy meeting place by changing the name of the pub to the Old Gipsy House or even the Old Gipsy Queen. This was taken a stage further in the 1880s by the aptly named John Cheater, who called it Ye Old Gipsy Queen.

The first Gipsy Tavern in 1875. (Lambeth Archives)

The second Gipsy Tavern in 1999.

This was in spite of the fact that the pub had been rebuilt in the late 1870s. The Gipsy Tavern was severely damaged by a V1 flying bomb on 3 August 1944, when Alfred S. Cassell was the landlord, and not reopened until 1950. The repaired building was simplified, with the ornate 1870s roof dispensed with. The pub was still the Old Gipsy House after the reopening, but since then it has adopted its present far more sensible name.

THE GLADSTONE, NO.167 PORTLAND ROAD

The pub was built during Gladstone's first spell as prime minister, and at the time of his greatest general popularity. Although the name is not recorded until 1874, there is no reason to doubt that it was used from the first. In 1869 it was described in a directory as 'a hotel to let'. By 1870 it was a beerhouse run by William Collier. The longest-serving landlord in the early years was Alfred Smith, who was there for more than a decade either side of 1900. Though it continued to be only a beerhouse it later proved more attractive to the landlords. Henry T. Read and J.H. Wheller served between them from the First to the Second World War. During much of the twentieth century the pub was known as the Gladstone Arms, but it has now reverted to its original style. It is a prominent landmark because it is taller than the neighbouring shops and houses, and stands on the bend of Portland Road.

GOAT HOUSE FARM, SUNNY BANK

It was quite common in the eighteenth century for farms to double as inns. It might have been suspected on general principles that this was the case with the ancient Goat House Farm, as it was later replaced by a pub, but there is also the direct confirmation that in 1817 Thomas

The Gladstone in 1998.

Goat House Farm in 1845. (Croydon Local Studies Library)

Allen, 'of The Goat House, Norwood, victualler', took out a Sun Fire Office insurance policy. A licenced victualler is of course a publican. The Allen family was at the farm for many years up to 1839. The later farmers, who did not necessarily continue with the inn-keeping side of the business, were Joshua Bull and his widow, followed by George Newman and a Mr Sparshott (perhaps William Sparshott from the Californian Tea Garden), who was there in 1859. The farm was demolished at about the time the Goat House Hotel was built, although they were not on the same site. The farm stood south-west of the pub, between what is now Regina Road and Sunny Bank. Regina Road was built (as Queen's Road) from 1863.

THE GOAT HOUSE HOTEL, NO.2 PENGE ROAD

In 1863 George Ingersent, a builder who had obtained a lease of the twenty-five acres of Goat House Farm from the Ecclesiastical Commissioners, and spent nearly £23,000 on building a tavern there, applied for a full licence for this splendid newcomer. He was refused because there were already four licenced houses and two beer shops in the immediate vicinity, but he tried again the next year and was successful. This was the debut of the Goat House Hotel, which immediately took rank as one of the leading public houses of South Norwood. It was an imposing three-storey building with attics. At the south end there was a tower that must have been a wonderful eyrie for a train spotter. At the north end was a single-storey wing that probably housed the public bar.

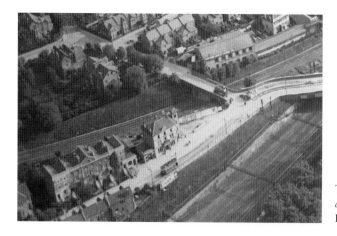

The first Goat House Hotel, centre, *c.*1924. (Croydon Local Studies Library)

The second Goat House Hotel in 1998.

George Ingersent (whose name is sometimes spelt Ingersant) no doubt meant to sell the lease and transfer the licence as soon as possible. He had a complicated business relationship with the hotel projector James Franks (of the Queen's and Clarendon Hotels), who must have seemed the perfect man to take over the Goat House. But the manager put in by Franks, one Thomas Paine, almost immediately took the liberty of stealing a cargo of wheat from Norwood Junction, and in the resulting scandal and confusion Ingersent was forced to resume direct responsibility for the pub. He did not live at the Goat House, but at No. 1 Bedford Villas, Penge Road, one of the many houses he had already built on the farm. That did not please the magistrates, who in 1866 warned him that he must take up residence in the pub, as the bench 'could not renew the licence to builders who lived elsewhere'. Rather than do that, Ingersent installed one J.B. Osborne, the third of a long line of landlords, none of whom stayed for long.

The ones who left their mark were J.F. and A.S. Barnes, who were in charge before and after the Goat House was rebuilt in 1936. It was certainly quixotic to rebuild a pub, especially one next to a railway bridge and junction, when the country was seriously threatened with war, but somehow the Goat House managed to come unscathed through the bombing. Perhaps it used up all its luck in doing so, for recently it has not been so fortunate. The pub was burnt out while under refurbishment on the night of the 14/15 July 1996. It was restored and reopened later that year, but closed again in 2003. Now the Goat House seems set for demolition and redevelopment. The saddest point is that its disappearance may involve the loss of one of Norwood's oldest place names. A comical link with the area's history was maintained until the 1990s (when the garden was turned into a car park) by the keeping of a pair of goats at the pub.

THE GREYHOUND, NO.14 HOLLAND ROAD

The Greyhound Tavern, one of Norwood's most attractive and distinctive pubs, was built in 1868. Until a few years earlier there had been only open country between the bend in Portland Road and Woodside Green, but now the Enmore Park estate was springing up to the west of Portland Road, and several enterprising developers responded by building pubs to serve the new population. The Prince of Denmark, the Spread Eagle, the Greyhound and the Gladstone were opened within a few years within a short distance of one another. The projector of the Greyhound was Edward Van Vliet, who later built many of the big houses in Selhurst Road, and in Lawrie Park Road at Sydenham. Here in Holland Road he suffered a rare setback when his

The Greyhound Tavern
in 1998.

The Hamilton Arms, *c.1921*. (Lambeth Archives)

application for a full licence was refused in 1869. He apparently cut his losses and moved on to greater things, for it was other men who applied unsuccessfully in later years. The longest-serving landlord was John Perrie Gordon, who was in charge for more than ten years during the 1880s and 1890s. The Greyhound closed a year or two ago, and its future now seems in doubt.

THE HAMILTON ARMS, NO.1 CLIVE ROAD

This pub at the corner of Clive Road and Hamilton Road was built in the 1850s, when both roads were new. The first publican I can discover is Robert Nelson Austin, who was 'formerly of the Hamilton Arms, Hamilton-road, beerseller' when bankrupt in 1859. The next is Charles Burtwell, who was there in 1860. He soon gave up beer selling to become a plumber & glazier, in which trade he was established in Hamilton Road (and the Old Kent Road) by 1861. After a brief appearance by Mrs Esther Baker in the early 1860s, the Hamilton Arms was run by Philip, or Pip, West from 1864 until 1914. That wide expanse of time was not filled by a single man, but by a father and son. The son, Philip Charles West, had a fling with the Paxton Tavern in 1901, while his younger brother Alexander managed the Hamilton Arms for him, but he soon returned to his first love. The last landlord was Albert Frederick Jeffree.

The Hamilton Arms closed in 1935, and in 1938 a block of flats known as Eaton Court was built on the site. The pub was one of the countless victims of the 1904 Licensing Act, which allowed magistrates to suppress pubs they considered superfluous by compensating the owners. This had a particularly strong effect in London between the wars, when brewers were persuaded to surrender the licences of several of their smaller and older houses in return for the grant of a new licence for a pub in an expanding suburb.

THE HOLLY BUSH, NO.2 WESTOW HILL

There was a squatter's cottage on this site at the corner of Westow Hill and Westow Street before the enclosure of the Croydon part of Norwood common in 1797. It was occupied by William Gardiner, who, as the cottage was then less than twenty years old, had to buy the freehold from the enclosure commissioners for £1 3s d. Gardiner continued to live there until the 1820s. After that the house, enlarged and improved, was occupied by Thomas Marlow until the mid-1830s. There is no indication that either of these men ran a pub. The Beer Act of 1830 allowed almost anyone to turn his house into a beer shop on payment of a 2 guinea annual excise fee. Charles White, the next owner of this prominent corner house, was one of thousands who took advantage of this new right. He was established there as a beer seller by 1838, and the sign was probably the Holly Bush from the start. It certainly was by 1839.

The original pub was very different from the present stately building. Its appearance in the early 1850s was recalled in the memoirs of Elizabeth Dee:

> The Holly Bush, standing back from the road, the front door was round the corner in Westow Street, with a latch to press down like an ordinary back door, there were a few funny little settles in front of the window and as you turned into Westow Street there was a very stunted holly bush in a corner.

The most notable of White's early successors was Henry Gillingham, landlord from 1841 to 1853. He had probably begun his local career at the Rising Sun in Spa Hill, and after his spell

J. E. ABRAHAMS.
"YE OLDE HOLLY BUSH HOTEL" WESTOW
HILL, UPPER NORWOOD.
SPECIAL DINNERS 1/- TEAS ETC. ETC.

The second Holly Bush,
c.1910.

at the Holly Bush he certainly continued it at the White Lion in South Norwood Hill. It was the ambition of every beerhouse keeper to obtain a licence to sell wines and spirits also, but the magistrates were chary of allowing these promotions. Gillingham failed to obtain one for the Holly Bush, and decamped to the fully licenced White Lion.

The Holly Bush was run by Henry Finch until his death in 1862, and by other members of the Finch family (who were later at the Queen's Arms in Westow Hill) until 1874. It was at the beginning of the Finch period, in the spring of 1853, that the pub was rebuilt on a much larger scale (as we know it today) and a full licence was achieved. The head lease was by this time held by Watney & Co., and the Finches were their tenants. There seems no doubt about the rebuilding date, as the rateable value of the Holly Bush rose from £27 in December 1852 to £225 in 1853. But there is a mystery connected with the subject because the 1847 map of Croydon, perhaps just in error, shows this corner plot as vacant. Yet it was undoubtedly the old building that Elizabeth Dee saw in the early 1850s.

The Holly Bush was very much a hotel in the years after the rebuilding. For the winter season of 1857 Henry Finch offered these reduced prices, 'Drawing rooms 10s 6d per week; bed rooms the same, including fires and lights. There is a handsome coffee room for the use of single gentlemen.' The Finches were followed by Richard Goodchild from 1874-86. In the twentieth century the licence of the Holly Bush was held for fifty-two years by members of the Abrahams family until the retirement of Philip and Clarence Abrahams in 1956. Victor Hucknall, a retired policeman who held the licence in the 1970s and 1980s, distinguished himself by regularly winning Watney's best kept cellar award.

The Hope, No.49 Norwood High Street

The Hope was built between 1840-43. It was empty in 1843, which might suggest it had just been completed. The owner was then George Tindall. The brewer's records go back only to 1850, so the early years are rather obscure, but the pub looks purpose-built rather than something cobbled together from existing cottages, and it is likely that the present Hope is the only one there has been. Thomas Samuel Long, the sole beer retailer listed in the High Street in 1845, was probably the first landlord of the Hope.

Prominent successors have been Edmund Stevenson from the early 1860s to the late 1870s, James Keniston from the early 1880s to 1912, Frank Newton, a refugee from the extinguished Forester's Arms, from 1914-23, and Ernest Arthur Smith from 1925-53.

The Hope moved towards its present appearance in 1936, when a rear extension was built, the original brickwork was rendered and whitewashed, and new windows were opened in the Pilgrim Hill flank wall. The extension included the first internal lavatories. Until then the customers used the urinal in Pilgrim Hill, which was considered very much as a public convenience. It caused endless trouble, especially in 1904, when the council threatened to oppose the renewal of the licence unless it was improved. Its removal in 1936 must have been a relief to all parties.

A pub the size of the Hope could not seriously aspire to a full licence, but in the 1880s the landlords did briefly describe themselves as wine and beer retailers.

The Horns, No.40 Knights Hill

It would take a very intelligent or lucky stranger to identify Norwood's oldest pub from modern appearances, but although it now looks sadly modern, cramped, and undistinguished, that honour probably belongs to the Horns in Knights Hill. There have been at least three buildings on the site. Thomas Frost remembered that the one demolished in the 1850s had an

The Hope from the railway bridge in 1936.

inscription recording that James I stopped there while stag hunting. One would not attach too much weight to that evidence, but the name of the pub and its location on the edge of the Great North Wood might well indicate that it was used by hunters as a convenient meeting place. A substantial building is shown on the site on a plan of the common made in 1678. In front of it is what appears to be a green surrounded by trees. The Horns certainly existed by the 1740s, as it is named on John Rocque's map. The way in which he places the lettering suggests that the name was also applied to the group of houses that had grown up beside the pub, on the edge of the common, since 1678.

The earliest landlord of whom we have a record is also the most interesting, not on his own account, but on that of his daughter. Robert Catley was a hackney coachman who plied his trade in and around Tower Hill, and so he would probably have remained but for the musical and sexual precocity of his daughter Ann Catley (1745-89), who from entertaining the officers at the Tower went on to be one of the most popular singers and actresses of the eighteenth century. Her success was exploited by a series of singing teachers, actor-managers, and lecherous aristocrats, but her father got his hands on enough of her earnings to retire from the cab stand and take a lease of the Horns. He is first recorded there in 1779 (see the Old Gipsy House) and last in 1785. It is most unlikely that Ann Catley ever lived at the pub. From 1768 until her death she was the mistress of Lt.-Col. Francis Lascelles, by whom she had at least eight children.

In the late eighteenth century the owner of the Horns was John Burgess. After Robert Catley his tenants were Benjamin Stevens (or Stephens) in 1786 and 1787, Benjamin Packwood in 1788, and William Packwood from 1791-1805. In their day, before the enclosure of the common, the inn was a very lonely place, and therefore a suitable rendezvous for those planning to fight a duel. Later licensees of the old Horns included Catherine Bocking in the 1820s, Alexander Hicks, William Hallows and George Butcher in the 1830s, Richard James Thompson Davis and his widow Elizabeth in the 1840s, and George Roe in the early 1850s. In 1848, when a seventy-two-year lease was for sale, it was described as 'the well-known house called the Horns, a capital country public-house'.

The old Horns was doomed by Act of Parliament, when the London, Brighton, & South Coast Railway obtained powers to build the West End & Crystal Palace Line. West Norwood Station was opened, as Lower Norwood, in December 1856. The cutting opposite the station, where the old Horns had stood, must have taken some time to dig, so the pub was probably demolished in 1855. Alfred Maudslay, the archaeologist, who was born in Norwood in 1850, had a curious anecdote in connection with this rebuilding. He wrote:

> I well remember the old country inn near the Norwood Cemetery, which stood back from the road with a row of pollarded lime-trees in front of it and a big swinging signboard, and I always ran past it fast, because the nursemaid told me a new railroad was coming through there, and I thought it might come dashing through at any moment.

There had been acres of land attached to the old pub. Most of what the railway company left was south-west of the track, far from Knights Hill and most unsuitable for a pub. This land was bought in 1859 as the site of the Jews' Hospital. That just left a small triangle of the original Horns yard squeezed between the north-east side of the cutting and Knights Hill, and it was here that the new pub was built between 1856-60. It was a plain two-storey building of no architectural interest. Thomas Wood (probably the one who was at the Railway Castle, in 1855) is the first landlord recorded for the new pub.

Above: The demolition of the second Horns in 1937. (Upper Norwood Joint Library)

Right: The third Horns in 1998.

The most interesting of the later landlords was Henry Jupp (1841-89), who opened the batting for Surrey from 1862-81, and twice turned out for England. He was at the Horns from 1875-78. The dominant name in the twentieth century was Pinchon. William Henry Pinchon was landlord from 1925-28, followed by Mrs Jessie Agnes Pinchon from 1929-51, and Donald Pinchon until at least 1958. It was in 1937, during Jessie Pinchon's tenure, that the Horns was rebuilt again as we know it today, in a style that is at least more attractive than that of the Victorian pub.

THE IVY HOUSE, KNIGHT'S HILL

W.T. Phillips recalled in 1842:

> Between Canterbury-grove and the Vicarage garden, whose site is now obliterated by the Public Library and the adjoining shops, the Press printing works, and part of Bloom-grove, stood a small beer-shop called the Ivy House. Here car men were wont to stop preparatory to whipping their horses up the hills that lay before them, and probably to whip up themselves for the occasion.

Beer shops sprang up everywhere after the Beer Act of 1830. Thomas Flint was the keeper of this one from 1836 or a little earlier until the 1840s. Perhaps the building of the Thurlow Arms across the road at the end of the decade forced its closure. By 1851 William Harknett, a fruiterer, and William Freeman, a carpenter, had divided the building between them as Nos 1 and 2 Ivy House. The description of the site given by Phillips is unintentionally a little confusing because the places he mentions – the library, Bloom Grove, etc. – were built over the vicarage garden, not on the site of the pub. The present Nos 366-372 Norwood Road mark the position of the Ivy House.

THE JOHN BULL, WEST NORWOOD

The 'John Bull, Lower Norwood' is the address given by a coachman seeking work, in an advertisement published in February 1853. It sounds like a beerhouse, places often used by servants as accommodation addresses, but I cannot say where this one stood.

THE JOINER'S ARMS, NOS 50 AND 52 WOODSIDE GREEN

The Joiner's Arms was the underdog at Woodside Green, overshadowed by the older and larger Beehive across the road, and restricted to a beer only licence during all its early history, but now at least it looks more attractive than its crudely modernised rival. The name seems surprising at first sight, given that the founder of the pub, Richard Winter, was a grocer & tobacconist on the site until he converted his shop into a beerhouse, probably in 1866. But in the 1871 census he is listed as a carpenter, even though his address is the Joiner's Arms, suggesting that both the grocer's shop and the beerhouse were mere sidelines in the early days.

Winter remained in charge until the late 1870s, when he left to found the even smaller Sidney Arms. The address in his time was No.1 Woodside Terrace; the No.50 was assigned in the early

The Joiner's Arms, *c.*1910. (John Gent)

1890s. The grocer's shop next door, the inheritor of Richard Winter's original sideline, was No.52. The pub incorporated the grocer's shop in 1901, and that is no doubt when the Joiner's Arms took on something like its modern appearance. No major rebuilding seems to have been involved, merely the combination of the two old shops into the enlarged pub. Two well named beer sellers, George Butt and Frederick Brown, ran the Joiner's Arms from the 1890s to the 1930s, and the next licensees, Mr and Mrs J.L. Britter, were only a letter away from completing a curious treble.

THE JOLLY SAILOR, NO.64 SOUTH NORWOOD HIGH STREET

The Jolly Sailor may not be quite the oldest pub in South Norwood, if it is true that Goat House Farm doubled as an inn, but it was certainly the first purpose-built pub in the whole Croydon half of Norwood. On the Lambeth side of the border it was only preceded by the Horns, the Old Gipsy House and the Rose & Crown. It was also the first pub built on any of the newly enclosed lands of Norwood Common after the Croydon and Lambeth Enclosure Acts of 1797 and 1806. The pub was founded between 1806 and 1810, probably by John Gaywood, who was the publican in 1810. The name is supposed to allude (rather oddly) to the bargemen who worked on the adjoining Croydon Canal, which was opened in 1809. The garden of the original pub ran down to the canal path.

There is just a hint of a possibility that this unusual name may not have been firmly established at first. The pub is called the Jolly Sailor in the 1810 rate book. However, in the 1811 census returns for Croydon, where John Gaywood, victualler, is duly noted as living in the house, another name is perhaps attached. In the margin, apparently in the same handwriting, is the pencilled note 'W. Hart'. Is this short for White Hart? There could not be any confusion with the White Hart at Upper Norwood, which was established in the 1820s. If there was any doubt about the name it was soon laid to rest when a life-sized carving of a sailor clutching a foaming

The second Jolly Sailor, c.1920. (John Gent)

jug of ale was placed above the porch. Unfortunately there is disagreement about the date of the old painting that shows this striking sign. One source says 1815, another 1832. Landlords after John Gaywood included Thomas and then Benjamin Weller in the 1820s and 1830s, George Eaton in the 1830s and 1840s, Thomas Pascall junior (son of the local brick maker) in the late 1840s, and John Perkins from 1849-68. The owners during this period were Meux & Co., the brewers. Several members of the Meux family had lived in the area, one at the Old Spa House at the top of South Norwood Hill.

John Perkins probably stayed at the Jolly Sailor just long enough to see the destruction of the original building, for the pub was rebuilt in 1867-68 on only a fraction of its former site. That was a dismal period for pub design. The gracefulness of the early nineteenth century had been lost and the exuberance of the late Victorians had not yet appeared. The new Jolly Sailor was a very dull building. Over the next few years the shops between the pub and Grosvenor Road spread over what had been the extensive pleasure gardens. The successors to Perkins in the new house were a Charles and William Smith, who quickly got into trouble with the police for various offences. The next landlord stayed only very briefly, but made his mark by changing the name of the old pub. In 1874 he was listed as 'A. Holledge, Royal (late Jolly) Sailor'. This was presumably an allusion to the Duke of Edinburgh, Queen Victoria's second son, who used to take a string quartet to sea with him. Holledge quickly departed, but his new name persisted until 1888. The only long-serving landlords after the pub reverted to its old name were the Langfords, William then George, who were in charge from the First World War until the early 1930s.

The Kings Head, now Southern Pride, No.82 Norwood High Street

An eighty-year remainder lease of the King's Head was sold in 1839. If this was originally for the familiar ninety-nine-year term, that would take the building back to 1820 or thereabouts. It could not be much older, as this was the unenclosed common until 1806. The earliest occupant recorded is Henry Ingledew, who was living here by 1829 and remained until 1831. His name is unusual in the south, but not uncommon in the north-east, where several Henry Ingledews have been prominent. Whether this one was an innkeeper is not certain, but it may just be relevant that in 1824 an 'Ingledoo' was the tenant of Beaulieu Cottage in Westow Hill (where the Methodist church later stood, and now the supermarket) and that the owner of that house was William Briant, landlord of the Horns Tavern, Kennington. There is also the fact that a man stabbed to death by an umbrella in January 1830 had lived for about three years in, 'a small cottage next to the King's Head public-house … in the little village of Norwood', but there is another Norwood in London to confuse the issue. We are on firmer ground by 1832, when Isaac Scott of the King's Head, Norwood, Surrey, is listed in a directory. By 1836 the licence had passed to William Mabley, and the King's Head continued in the Mabley family until the early 1850s. We get a glimpse of the inn at this period from the report of a court case in 1845:

> Between 1 and 2 o'clock on Wednesday the prisoners drove up to the King's Head Tavern at Norwood in a gig, and went into the house. The women went upstairs into a bed-room, but were afterwards shown into a room on the ground floor, where they had half a pint of gin. The landlady, Mrs Mobley, however, saw the prisoner Robinson, who was dressed in a riding habit, with a hat and long veil, come down stairs and leave the house in a hurried manner. This excited her suspicions, and caused her to go up to her bed-room, where she missed from her drawers a piece of satin. She instantly hurried down stairs, and sent the potman after the prisoner to request she would return, but instead of doing so, she was going on towards town, and was ultimately taken into custody and brought back to the King's Head. On being accused of taking the satin, she replied, 'If I have stolen it, I must have been dreaming;' but the daughter of Mrs Mobley and another witness distinctly saw the prisoner throw the satin into a ditch, from which it was taken. The male prisoner, upon the accusation of felony being made against his companion, became most violent, struck the landlady and her daughter, and also the policeman.

It was a feature of this prominent and popular inn that (until it was rebuilt) the landlords served for long periods. The successor to the Mableys, Alfred Charles Drouet, was at the King's Head from the early 1850s until the late 1870s. Wilson says he was known as Doctor Drouet. 'This was because he always knew a remedy for all ills. For instance anyone asking for a drop of rum for a cold would be told, "You don't want rum, take this home and try it". "This" being some remedy of his own.'

The inn had several features that set it apart from the run of Norwood pubs. Behind it lay the Tivoli Gardens, where, as Thomas Frost remembered, 'stood a maze and a small menagerie, and on the lawn of which I heard Robert Owen lecture on The Rational System of Society, on the occasion of a muster of his disciples from Lambeth and Southwark.' W.T. Phillips remembered the maze: 'Contrary to the maternal orders, I once entered, and racing round the thorny convolutions of the maze, discovered later on its effect on a new pair of trousers that I

Above: The first King's Head, *c.*1875. (Lambeth Archives)

Left: The second King's Head in the 1920s.

was wearing; a rent, all too evident of my disobedience.' Wilson adds cricket, quoits, and skittles to the list of attractions offered by the Tivoli Gardens. They were entered via an archway to the left of the inn.

To the right was the entrance to the music hall, a large extension at the back probably built specially for the purpose in the 1850s. The King's Head had a music licence from 1857-91, and used it to put on plays as well as variety. Wilson mentions 'thrilling dramas such as *Sweeney Todd*, *East Lynne*, etc.', and Thomas Frost remembered seeing 'a performing tiger act a prominent part in a sensational drama setting forth the perils of a British traveller in Africa'. The old King's Arms had a forecourt where stalls were set up (like the ones seen more recently at the Thurlow Arms) for the sale of toffee and other delicacies, and a band would play on Saturday nights. The inn also 'formed the terminus to all the Norwood omnibuses' as Alfred Drouet alleged in his defence in 1865, when hauled before the bench 'for serving suspect bona-fide travellers'. How could he tell the true from the false amid such a throng of callers? Readers of *The Diary of a Nobody* will recall poor Mr Pooter's difficulties with this notoriously elastic rule about serving travellers with drinks out of hours.

The great days of the King's Head, like those of many another old suburban inn, ended when the owners foolishly decided to rebuild. The result was a featureless box flush with the road, so that the forecourt, such a feature of local life, was lost. What had been the picturesque goal of an outing became just another pub, with nothing to distinguish it from 1,000 rivals. This happened at the King's Head in 1891, when the music hall licence was surrendered, and billiards became the new attraction. Since then there is nothing much to record, except a succession of quickly changing landlords, some with unusual names, like Arthur Charles Savigear (1938-39) and O.U. Millest (1951-52). There were major internal alterations in 1936, and again in 1957. In 1998 another owner made another foolish decision by changing the name of this old pub to Southern Pride.

THE KNIGHT'S HILL TAVERN, NO.356 NORWOOD ROAD

Nos 362-354 Norwood Road, formerly known as Nos 1-5 Castle Place, are among the oldest shops in Norwood, in constant use as such since they were built in the 1830s. All have been greatly altered over the years, but none perhaps entirely rebuilt. Among the many trades that have flitted in and out of the five shops in those 170 years there have been at least two beer shops. A Mrs Frances Dixon ran the Knight's Hill Tavern at No.4 Castle Place, now No.356 Norwood Road, in 1864. By the next year she was listed as having a dairy at the same address, and as George Dixson had appeared as a cow keeper at the Knight's Hill Dairy, No.4 Castle Place, in 1863, it would appear that the tavern was a very short-lived experiment. It was probably killed off by the Railway Castle beerhouse which was only two doors away at No.2. The building is seen in the photograph of the former Railway Castle on p.86.

THE LONDON TAVERN, NO.158 CLIFTON ROAD

This obscure pub at the corner of Clifton Road and Whitehorse Lane, apparently began as an off-licence, blossomed into the London Tavern for fifteen or twenty years, and then subsided into an off-licence once more. The earliest reliable trace of it is in 1878, when W. Beal is recorded at 'ale stores, Clifton Road'. That probably indicates an off-licence, though 'stores' was sometimes

The former London Tavern in 1998.

used in pub names, in Scotland more often than in England. By 1884 Edward J. Barnes is listed here at the London Tavern.

It continued as a pub at least until 1899, when Mrs E.C. Blake was the landlady, but by 1902 Albert Samuel Blake had turned it into an off-licence again, even though he was still calling it the London Tavern. That must have caused confusion, so a later proprietor, E.A.P. Richards, changed the name to the London Stores. Yet a 1958 directory records 'Albert E. Pennington Richards, London Tavern', so perhaps the old name was still displayed somewhere on the premises. The Richards family continued to run the business until at least 1968. The building still stands and looks entirely like a typical corner pub. It is now divided into flats.

THE LORD NELSON, SOUTH NORWOOD HIGH STREET

Peter Walker says that there was a pub of this name on the north side of South Norwood High Street in 1855, when it was 'untenanted'. I have not been able to find this reference, or any other trace of this sign.

THE MASONS' ARMS, NO.12 OR 14 GIPSY HILL

In April 1860 there was an advertisement for the sale of a small estate in Gipsy Hill, 'near to the railway station', by the executors of John Carpenter.

> It comprises the Masons' Arms Beerhouse, in the occupation of Mr Dangerfield, at a rental of £40 per annum; also a Baker's Shop (with possession), with plate-glass front and dwelling house

Gipsy Hill around 1917 showing Nos 12 and 14
(beyond the police station), one of them
formerly the Mason's Arms.

over, estimated to be let at a rental of £40 per annum, held upon lease for 90½ years, wanting
seven days, from the 25th day of June 1856, at a peppercorn rent.

The Lambeth rate book for May 1860 lists Edward Dangerfield in Gipsy Hill for a house and
premises with a rateable value of £33. (This rate does not distinguish private dwellings from
shops or pubs, calling them all houses.) The position of the Dangerfield entry, between the police
station (now No.10a) and the Methodist chapel (now No.16) suggests that the beerhouse and
baker's shop were at Nos 12 and 14, but as the shop is not included in the rate book, presumably
because it was still empty, it is impossible to tell which was which. The 1861 census shows both
shops as unoccupied. The Masons' Arms was evidently a short-lived enterprise. In 1859 there
was a Mr E.J. Dangerfield, architect, at '1 Gipsy-hill', which would then have meant the nearest
house to Westow Hill on the east side. If an architect decided to found a pub, the Masons' Arms
would be an appropriate name.

THE NORFOLK COURT HOTEL, NO.315 BEULAH HILL

I had not intended to include the Norfolk Court, as it was more akin to a modern bed and
breakfast establishment than a traditional licenced hotel, but its recent demolition gains it
a sentimental place. It stood on the site of one of the old houses of Norwood, occupied
by several generations of the Howard family from the first years of the nineteenth century.
Although they had no connection with the ducal Howards a flattering friend suggested that
they adopt the name Norfolk House, which they did from the early 1870s. Rupert Montague-
Browne, the flatterer's son, remembered that, 'Norfolk House has been quite transmogrified,
and this since the disastrous fire in our friends the Misses Howards' time.' The last

Miss Howard was listed there until 1884. The fire was perhaps in 1882, when there was an auction of the contents.

The rebuilt or remodelled house was in a heavy style, with much use of red hanging tiles. Its most notable owner was James Epps junior, of the cocoa family, who was there for about fourteen years until his early death in 1905. Norfolk House, somewhat enlarged to fit it for the new role, became the Norfolk Court Hotel in the early 1970s. It was demolished with unseemly haste in December 2005.

THE NORWOOD HOTEL, NO.3 KNIGHTS HILL

The opening of a new railway station was always a rallying call to speculators in pubs and hotels. The fact that the creation of Lower Norwood Station (opened in 1856) had involved the near extinction of the Horns, the venerable local inn, made the prospect even more tempting. The shrunken Horns had struggled back into existence by 1860, and for a few years had the railway business almost to itself, but then the grand shape of the Norwood Hotel began to rise across the road, almost adjoining the station, and the Horns was permanently overshadowed. The shift in the balance of power was emphasised by the fact that the first recorded landlord of the hotel, in 1864, was a deserter to the enemy. Joseph Sargent had held the licence of the Horns in 1863, but evidently decided that prospects looked better on the other side of the street.

Few of the early landlords stayed for long. Henry Osborne, who was in charge from 1880-86, is the only exception. Things improved in the twentieth century, when John William Smith was landlord from 1919-35, and Roland (or Rowland) Walker from 1936-49. Like many other finely

Opposite: The Norfolk Court Hotel in 1995.

Right: The Norwood Hotel, *c.*1910. (John Gent)

detailed Victorian buildings, the Norwood Hotel survives today in a sadly diminished state. Over many decades accident, neglect, and economy have robbed it of features that gave energy and variety to the original design, but even now it is one of the most striking of Norwood pubs.

THE NO.1, NO.1 DUNBAR PLACE

This back-street pub with the curious name stood at the corner of what are now Dunbar Place and Dunbar Street. For most of its existence, however, it had the address No.1 Wood Street, and in its earliest days it was described as being in Elm Grove. That was the name of the old Norwood house, for many years a private boys' school, that was demolished in 1861, and on the site of which and its elm grove dozens of little houses were built in the 1860s. That is the earliest possible date for the pub, but in fact there is no sign of it in the 1871 census. The first likely reference is in an 1872 directory, where Thomas Morley is listed as a beer retailer in Elm Grove. An 1874 directory gives a similar description for one Parks Hope. These were probably the first two landlords of the No.1.

Certainty is reached in 1876 with Henry Caldcleugh. He remained for ten years, which was long enough for his address to change from Elm Grove to No.1 Wood Street. We learn something of the value of a small back street pub from the sale of the No.1 Beerhouse, Dunbar Street, in August 1894. The rent paid by the landlord was then £40 per annum, and the price realised for the freehold was £600. Wilson records that the No.1 was closed by the licensing magistrates in June 1935, under the terms of the Licensing Act of 1904. '*Are we to part like this,*

The No.1 in the 1920s. (Lambeth Archives)

Bill? was sung by its old customers as its doors closed for the last time as a tribute to Mr William Hartwell, who ministered to the thirst of his neighbours there for twenty-eight years. 'The old pub appears to have been divided into two houses as Nos 1 and 1a Dunbar Place. As such it survived heavy wartime bombing, but not the sweeping post-war clearances of all the turnings to the east of Norwood High Street.

THE OLD GIPSY HOUSE, GIPSY HILL

The title of oldest pub in Norwood belongs either to the Horns or the Old Gipsy House. In the eighteenth century, and perhaps earlier, these were the two places of entertainment on the London fringe of Norwood Common where visitors from the capital refreshed themselves before facing the climb up Knight's Hill or Gipsy Hill. One of the attractions of Norwood for these day-trippers was the fame of the Gipsy fortune tellers. Their headquarters was at Hall Green, on the edge of which stood the Old Gipsy House. The 1678 map of the common shows a house on or near this site, so it is not impossible that this was the spot on which Elizabeth Pepys had her fortune told in 1668, as disapprovingly recorded by her husband in his diary. 'This afternoon, my wife and Mercer and Deb went with Pelling to see the Gypsies at Lambeth and have their fortunes told; but what they did, I did not enquire.' The house on the 1678 map is most likely to be the ancestor of the Oaks, which stood just north of the Gipsy House, but it is quite possible that the pub was founded at the Oaks and moved to a new building nearby when that was converted into a gentleman's house.

The Old Gipsy House in 1802. (Croydon Local Studies Library)

The earliest record of the landlords of both the Old Gipsy House and the Horns comes from an account of a trial in 1779, in which one Humphrey Finnimore was accused of stealing five turkeys from Thomas Humphries of the Sign of the Gypsies at Norwood. Catley of the Horns appeared as a witness for the defence. In the 1780s Richard Newbery or Newberry is listed as the licensee of this pub, which was called the Gypsies in 1784, and the Gypsey House in 1786 and 1787. The only other landlord of whom I can find any record was probably the last. Edward Morris was there, as the tenant of Samuel Waring, between 1803 and 1807.

It was in 1806 that the Lambeth enclosure commissioners confirmed Samuel Waring's ownership of this piece of old enclosure on the common. Waring lived at the Oaks, just to the north of the pub. Like other respectable residents of the new suburb Waring was probably keen to get rid of the gypsies. Armed with his secure new title to the estate, he closed the pub and built a smart villa on its site, which he called Gipsy House. The rebuilding took place between 1807-23, when Greenwood's guide to the architectural features of the district records, 'Gipsey-House, an elegant small house ..., the seat of – Waring, Esq.'. Nobody could have described the old pub as 'elegant'. As seen in an 1802 engraving, it was a primitive wooden building, the upper floor projecting far forward supported by three posts. The new Gipsy House, which was sometimes occupied by members of the Waring family and sometimes let to tenants, survived until the late nineteenth century, when it had become No. 101 Gipsy Hill. It was rebuilt and renamed The Nook, and was later called Charters. Its position is taken today by Charters Close.

The Oxford Arms in 1967. (Lambeth Archives)

THE OXFORD ARMS, NO.2 NASEBY ROAD

The Oxford Arms was the largest and the most successful of the three Norwood New Town pubs. The others were the Eagle Tavern and the Fox under the Hill. When the Oxford Arms closed in 1967 reports gave its opening date as 1862. That is quite possibly when it was built, but the earliest reference I can find is to 'W. Abnett, Beerhouse, New Town', in the December 1863 rate book. He was not included in March 1863. An 1865 directory gives him as a beer retailer and builder, so it is likely that the Oxford Arms was his own work.

As William Alfred Abnett he applied for a full licence in March 1864, but the grant was opposed by the landlord of the nearby Eagle, and refused. Abnett tried again the next year, this time describing the Oxford Arms as, 'one of the prettiest little houses in the locality'. He told the magistrates that he had a ninety-nine-year lease, had made a previous application, and had been running the house without complaint. The magistrates were sufficiently impressed by this statement to resolve to view the premises, and the visit was clearly successful, as the licence was granted in March 1865. Abnett stayed until 1870. No other landlords served for so long until the Catt family took over in 1916. James Catt was the first, and Ron and Ivy Catt saw the Oxford Arms through to its closure and demolition in 1967, as part of the almost total clearance of Norwood New Town. A replacement was considered in the plans for redevelopment, but in the end only housing was built.

A View of Mrs. Nesbitts (late the Earl of Bristol's) Villa, near the Horns in Norwood
Publish'd by I. Sewell, in Cornhill, 1786.

Park House, later the Park Hotel, in 1786.

The Park Hotel, Central Hill

The career of this notable Norwood building as the Park Hotel was a brief interlude between longer and more eventful periods when it was a private house and a convent. As a house site it can be traced back at least to the late seventeenth century, but the present building was created in the 1760s by Alexander Nesbitt, and enlarged by his widow Mary Nesbitt and her lover, the third Earl of Bristol. Mrs Nesbitt was much abroad between 1814 and her death in 1825, and Park House was let. In 1824 and 1825 the tenants were Scott & Co., who may possibly have been hoteliers. If so, the house reverted to private use until 1831.

From 1 January 1832 it was taken by Richard Wright, who set about converting it into what was described in an August 1832 advertisement as 'Norwood-park Hotel, the intended new and splendid hotel in the centre of Norwood-park'. The triumphant opening of the Beulah Spa pleasure grounds in 1831 had created a demand for hotel accommodation in the vicinity. Wright stayed for only a year, and probably never entertained a guest, for in April 1833 it was announced that 'Mr Mollard (late of the Crown & Sceptre, Greenwich) having fitted up the Park Mansion, Norwood, as an hotel for company visiting the Beulah Spa, is now ready for the reception of the public', and in August that Mollard's Grand Hotel in the Norwood Park had already opened, and that unequivocal success had marked its progress. John Mollard was the author of a popular manual, *The Art of Cookery* (1801), of which a new edition appeared in 1836. Mollard died suddenly on a Fulham omnibus in 1838. By then he had sold the hotel to Charles Crawley, who was to remain until 1845, and his name for considerably longer.

There was some excitement at the hotel in 1840, when Sir Francis Burdett and his daughter Angela Burdett Coutts, the great heiress, were among the guests. Miss Coutts was being stalked by an Irish fortune hunter named Richard Dunn, who followed her to St Luke's church and in all her walks around Norwood. She was, 'frequently obliged to quit the private grounds of the hotel' because Dunn appeared 'in the road and fields contiguous to the hotel and overlooking the grounds, continually annoying and alarming her by waving his pocket handkerchief, and making gestures at her'. Charles Crawley and two of his waiters were sued by Dunn after they forcibly ejected him from the grounds. Dunn claimed that 'he heard Mr Crawley exclaim that he deserved to be thrown into the horse pond; this was in the road opposite to the hotel'. Crawley was acquitted, but the case had the unfortunate result that these fashionable guests beat a hasty retreat, and the reputation of the hotel was damaged.

Charles Crawley persevered until 1848. In October of that year the furniture, farming stock, and effects of the Park Hotel were advertised for sale. The declining fortunes of the Beulah Spa must have harmed the business, and the Crystal Palace did not arrive soon enough to save it.

The house was bought for the Convent of the Faithful Virgin which, with its school, remains in occupation to this day. Park House was seriously damaged during the Second World War, but was patched up, and survives as part of the convent. When Rupert Montague Browne visited it early in the twentieth century he noticed a relic of the hotel. 'Over the portal of the front door is the name Crowley in black lettering - and this, the good nuns told me, could not be obliterated, but appeared again and again, bobbed up serenely (they didn't say that!) or ever the workmen effaced the inscription.'

THE PARK TAVERN, NO.56 ELDER ROAD

The original address of The Park Tavern, current until the First World War, was No.3 Maudslay's Cottages. The Maudslay in question was Thomas Henry Maudslay, the engineer, of Holderness House, Knight's Hill, who built this terrace at the bottom of his long garden in the late 1850s. The site of Holderness House is now the recreation ground in Knight's Hill. The pub has been rebuilt, but until 1924 it was housed in two cottages identical to the ones that survive next door. The pub was probably founded immediately the cottages were built, for 'James Whitehead, beer retailer, Park Road' is listed in an 1860 directory. He remained until 1872, by which time the Park Tavern name was well established. It was a beer shop then, and continued to be so until the distinction faded away in the middle of the twentieth century. The only other long-serving landlords have been Daniel Vail and his widow from 1916-34, and Frederick Walter Bliss from 1935 until at least 1958. The rebuilding in 1924 was a rare example of one that has improved the appearance of a pub, and the Park Tavern is now one of the best-looking houses in the district. The architect was Charles Miller of Chancery Lane.

THE PAXTON ARMS, NO.52 ANERLEY HILL

The Paxton Arms is one of the many pubs founded in Norwood during the 1850s in the hope of profiting from the Crystal Palace boom. Here the position and name of the pub make the connection explicit. It was probably built in 1855 or 1856, but the first landlord I can identify is James Careless, who was installed by 1860, and remained until 1865. It sounds an unpromising name, but it was Careless's successor who came to grief at the Paxton Arms.

Above: The first Park Tavern, *c.* 1910. (Lambeth Archives)

Right: The second Park Tavern in 1999.

The Paxton Arms, *c.*1903.

Frederick Carver Marshall, who described himself as a wine and spirit merchant, was bankrupt by May 1867. This may have set the tone, for of all the numerous Victorian landlords only the last stayed for more than a few years. Thomas George Wernham and his widow Mrs Fanny Laura Wernham clocked up some twenty years' service between them from 1898. The Paxton Arms was wrecked by a flying bomb in 1944. Its condition at the end of the war can be seen in the photograph of the damaged Rising Sun. om p.88. The pub was finally reopened, with the interior completely remodelled, in December 1955. The first landlord of the restored Paxton Arms was H.A. Warren.

THE PAXTON TAVERN NOW THE MANSION, NO.255 GIPSY ROAD

The Paxton Tavern occupies a dominant position on the boundary of Norwood and Dulwich, and at the meeting point of seven roads. Of all the many Crystal Palace-inspired pubs this was the first in the field. It existed by August 1853, nearly a year before the official opening of the palace. At first the new pub's *raison d'etre* was made even more obvious, for its original name was the Palace Hotel & Tavern. An advertisement for it under that name in June 1854 recommends the delightful walk to the Palace 'along the new road through Dulwich Wood', which we now know as Dulwich Wood Park. In the following month a notice directed to omnibus proprietors drew attention to the good stabling for twenty-four horses at the Palace Hotel & Tavern, at the foot of Gipsy Hill. At that period William Rowlett was the landlord. The name had been changed to the Paxton Hotel & Tavern by January 1855, when there was much boasting about the new billiard table, and a year later the advertisement was for 'the Paxton Hotel, Norwood, enlarged & improved, William Leeks, late cook to the Earl of Zetland, proprietor'.

Of the many later licensees the ones who served longest were Rowland Henry Wallis from 1876-98, Charles Rogers from 1910-30, and Ernest George Hayes from 1934 until his death in 1953. Ernie Hayes (1876-1953) was a celebrated Surrey all-rounder, a right-handed bat and leg-break bowler, who scored forty-eight first-class centuries and took over 500 wickets. He also appeared five times for England between 1906-12, but without much success. Hayes turned to innkeeping after a spell with Leicestershire and five years coaching at the Oval. After his death his widow ran the pub for a few years more. The Paxton still stands proudly in its fine position, but is now painted a gloomy black, and known as the Mansion. It is astonishing that anyone could prefer something so dull and meaningless to a name as historic and appropriate as the Paxton Tavern.

THE POSTAL ORDER, NO.33 WESTOW STREET

The Postal Order is one of Norwood's newest pubs, founded around 1998 by J.D. Wetherspoon, but it does occupy a building of some interest. No.35, next door, now Los Toreros. became the Norwood Chief District Post & Telegraph Office in 1884 or 1885. No.33, now the Postal Order, was added around 1893, and used as the postmen's sorting office.

The Paxton Tavern in the 1930s.

The Postal Order and Rockwell's (now Los Toreros) in 1995.

THE PRINCE OF DENMARK, NOW OCEANS APART, NO.152 PORTLAND ROAD

The four pubs in and around South Portland Road – the Prince of Denmark, the Gladstone, the Spread Eagle, and the Greyhound – were built with competitive speed between 1865-69, as the development of the Enmore Park Estate began the transformation of what had lately been an entirely agricultural area. The Prince of Denmark was the first in the field, in 1866. The date gives the clue to the origin of the name. Alexandra of Denmark had married the Prince of Wales in 1863. The pub was presumably named in honour of her brother, the Crown Prince of Denmark.

James Griffiths (or Griffith) was the first landlord, from 1866-71. He made an application for a full licence in 1866 and obtained one in the next year. It is curious that none of his successors exceeded the modest four-year tenure of the founder until Mrs A.V. Kernick clocked up some fifteen years in the 1920s and 1930s. The trend suggests a struggling pub, but perhaps all its licensees were making quick fortunes and retiring to a life of leisure. The lavish rebuilding of the Prince of Denmark in 1898 might suggest prosperity, but that was a decade when brewers were filled with unjustified optimism, and spent extravagantly to 'improve' their pub estates, often by

The Prince of Denmark in 1998.

replacing modestly attractive pubs with garish gin palaces. We cannot say that that was the case here, as we do not know what the original Prince was like, and the existing building is a good example of 1890s design. In recent years the pub has followed another and more deplorable trend. The name has been changed to the fatuous Oceans Apart.

THE PUZZLE, NOS 25 AND 27 WESTOW HILL

This is one of the newest Norwood pubs, founded around 1999, but the premises are much older. A semi-detached pair of houses known as Beulah or Beaulieu Place was built some way from the road, with good front gardens, probably in the 1830s. The two shops were built over the front gardens around 1884, and the first recorded use of No.25 was as dining rooms, in 1886. By 1888 it had become a chemist's shop, and so it remained until the 1990s. By contrast, No.27 was used for all manner of trades, never settling to one for very long until it was annexed by No.25. It is surprising that a new pub could obtain a licence here, as it is next door to the old-established Queen's Arms, Westow Hill.

Left: The Puzzle in 2000, with the Queen's Arms, Westow Hill, beyond.

Opposite above: The first Queen's Arms, Portland Road, *c.* 1910. (Croydon Local Studies Library)

Opposite below: The second Queen's Arms, Portland Road, in 1998.

THE QUEEN'S ARMS, NO.40 PORTLAND ROAD

This pub, now sadly closed and not looking likely to open again, is one of the oldest in South Norwood, although the existing premises are not original. The Queen's Arms was probably built in 1844-45 by John King, who was the owner-occupier in 1845. If King was the builder, the usual practice would have been for him to dispose of his pub as soon as he had established it. By 1849, certainly, and probably earlier, James Tart had become his tenant. He was in his early thirties when he took over the Queen's Arms, and he remained in charge until 1863. He began as a beer seller, but obtained a full licence around 1854.

A seventy-year remainder lease of the Queen's Head, Farley Road, South Norwood was sold for £15,500 in 1897, at the height of the pub boom. The rent was then £125 per annum. This was presumably the Queen's Arms as described by a very inaccurate reporter, as it then stood at the corner of Farley Road, which is now known as Doyle Road. The last landlord of the old Queen's Arms was Alfred William Rice, who was there from 1904-24.

The original building was more attractive and substantial than the present one, and exactly the same size, so it is hard to understand or forgive its rebuilding in 1924. That was just before the Butcher family took over the pub in 1926. They held the licence until at least the 1980s. The Queen's Arms was being called the Two Bobbys in the first years of the twenty-first century, from which any good judge could have predicted the approaching collapse. The pub was boarded-up and 'to let' by January 2005.

Left: The Queen's Arms, Westow Hill, in 1971. (Croydon Local Studies Library)

Opposite: The Queen's Hotel, *c.*1910.

THE QUEEN'S ARMS, NOW THE BLACK SHEEP, NO.23 WESTOW HILL

The building in which the Queen's Arms was established in the early 1850s was a house, possibly called Virginia Lodge, that had been occupied in the 1830s and 1840s by William Pocknell, the proprietor of the Westow Hill windmill. In the early 1850s the tenant of Virginia Lodge was 'William T. Imeson, B.A. of London University, and Professor of Languages' but by 1855 a directory includes 'Samuel Sheen, Queen's Arms, Westow hill'. He was bankrupt by early 1856, and Truman, Hanbury, & Co., the brewers, held the lease as security until a sale could be arranged. John Cox was the landlord in 1860 and 1861, and William Henry Collens and his widow Elizabeth held the licence during most of the 1860s.

In the early 1870s it was acquired by 'Henry Finch'. This was an early example of the public house chain, in the style, but not on the scale, of the modern J.D. Wetherspoon. By the 1930s it was known as Henry Finch Ltd. Wine was the centre of the Finch business, and the various pubs run under the banner were essentially wine bars. The headquarters was at the Old Holborn Bars in High Holborn, and after the Finches acquired the Queen's Arms in the 1870s that also came to be called the Old Holborn Bars more often than not. Henry Finch had been at the Holly Bush until the his death in 1862, after which it was run for a decade by other members of the Finch family, but their connection with it was severed at about the time they took over the Queen's Arms. That pub continued as part of the Henry Finch chain until 1956. Since then it has gone through an unhappy period marked by frequent refurbishments, with the changes of name so often linked with them. The pub was called The Orange Kipper in the late 1990s, was the Queen's Arms again by November 1999, but since 2004 has been the Black Sheep.

Queens Hotel, Upper Norwood.

THE QUEEN'S HOTEL, NO.122 CHURCH ROAD

The Queen's Hotel, much the largest licenced premises in Norwood, was the creation of 'the late Mr James Franks who, in his day, built largely in the neighbourhood', as Corbet Anderson recorded some forty years later. The building rose in 1853-54, at the same time as the Crystal Palace, its inspiration, and the Royal Crystal Palace Hotel, its main rival. The architect employed by Franks was Francis Pouget of Southwark. It is difficult now to appreciate his work, as the design has been butchered by unfortunate demolitions and extensions. It was always highly irregular, and incorporated at least one house already standing on the site. In 1854 the Queen's was described as 'these magnificent series of hotels built on a hill of gravel'. The first known manager was George Colleton Cooke. In 1855 James Franks was being assessed for rates at the colossal valuation of £600, but undeterred he continued to add to the amenities. In September 1855 he advertised 'Queen's Hotel and its Park: the delightful shrubbery park formerly belonging to Lady Williams is now added to this quiet family hotel. The nobility & gentry are especially invited to secure apartments or the wings before they require them.' The Park still exists opposite the Queen's Hotel, but since the 1860s it has been occupied by houses rather than strolling hotel guests. In 1856 Franks founded the Clarendon Hotel in Beulah Hill as an annex, and by 1859 extensions to the Queen's Hotel itself had taken the rateable value to £970. In March of that year an advertisement boasted that 'fifty more rooms have been added to this health-restoring establishment'. In 1861 advertisements for the Hotel de la Reine informed 'foreigners of distinction that during the past 12 months upwards of 100 rooms have been added to this palatial residence'.

With all this investment it is not surprising that by 1861 the Queen's Hotel Company Ltd had been formed, with Thomas Holt as manager until 1872. He had previously been at the now closed Clarendon Hotel. Fresh building continued: in 1881 an advertisement drew attention to the 'large banqueting hall, built especially for City and other companies' dinners'. The Queen's Hotel, which had long been in the habit of entertaining the nobility and gentry, had its finest hour in 1887 when the Crown Prince of Germany, later the Emperor Frederick III, stayed at the Queen's Hotel with the Crown Princess Victoria, daughter of the Queen. He was in London receiving treatment for cancer, but the doctors could do nothing for him, and he returned to Berlin to succeed and die. Another eminent guest was Émile Zola, who stayed at the Queen's Hotel in 1898-99, while in exile on account of his championship of Dreyfus.

Two later celebrities associated with the Queen's illustrate the decline of the hotel and the district in the twentieth century. With the Crystal Palace, its *raison d' être*, fading to oblivion, and fashion deserting Upper Norwood, the hotel had increasing difficulty in filling its many rooms. The management responded by converting parts of the building into flats. When Lawrence Durrell (1912-90) and his mother and brothers (including Gerald, 1925-95) returned from India around 1930, they faced the familiar Anglo-Indian problem of finding affordable accommodation in England. They lived first in a big house at Dulwich, and then 'in a flat above the Queen's Hotel'. The hotel is the shabby setting for Lawrence's novel, *The Black Book*, which was published in Paris in 1938.

The post-war history of the Queen's Hotel has been a catalogue of disasters. In the early 1970s the beautiful listed villa, The Tyrol, the hotel's northern neighbour in Church Road, was demolished to make way for an extremely undistinguished extension. Yet a few years later, when the south wing was seriously damaged by fire, the management sought permission to replace it with a nursing home. In 1977 Croydon mysteriously delisted the hotel long enough to give permission for its partial demolition, but when the damaged wing was removed in 1980 it was replaced not by a nursing home but by a car park. There was another destructive fire in 1981. In 1999 a manager with a sense of humour changed the name to the Quality Hotel. It happily became the Queen's Hotel again in 2003, but any real improvement in quality is still hard to detect. It is very sad, for there is enough remaining in this wreckage of a great hotel for something fine to be salvaged.

The Railway, No.7 Station Rise

The Railway cannot be older than 1868, when Tulse Hill Station was opened, but it clearly followed soon after, as Thomas Samuel Smith was the landlord by 1870. In a directory of that year his address is given rather oddly as 'Railway Tavern, Knight's Hill, Tulse Hill station'. The reference here is to the 'other' Knight's Hill, north of Thurlow Park Road. Smith had a good grounding in the business, for his father, also Thomas, was Secretary to the Licenced Victuallers' Society.

The founder remained in charge throughout the 1870s before handing over to another of the great family of Smiths. Henry Richardson Smith (not, I suppose, necessarily related) did even better, holding the licence until 1905. Later landlords have also tended to stay for long periods. Charles William Glanville was in charge from 1906-15, Herbert William Atkins and William Nicholas from 1931-42, and Arthur Brown from 1943 until at least 1958. All of these were beer retailers, as the pub did not obtain a full licence until after the Second World War. It has most often been called the Railway Tavern, with the Railway Hotel as an occasional variant. Both have now been dropped in favour of the Railway.

The Railway in 1998.

THE RAILWAY BELL, NO.14 CAWNPORE STREET

The founder of the Railway Bell was Harriet Wickenden, but the date is not quite certain. In 1861 she was the keeper of a lodging house in Gipsy Hill, not far from the station. The census described her as a married woman, but although she had a son and daughter (named Smith) living with her, there was no sign of a husband. By 1863 a directory lists her as, 'Mrs Harriet Wickenden, beer retailer, Gipsey hill' and in 1867 she is described as, 'Mrs Harriett Wickenden, Railway Bell, 3 Malta Cottages, Gipsy Hill'. There is little doubt that by 3 Malta Cottages was meant the present pub in Cawnpore Street, which at that time was known as George Street; it is just possible that Harriet Wickenden began her beer-selling career at her old address in Gipsy Hill before moving to the new Railway Bell around 1865. That is the building date given by Young & Co., the brewers, who bought the pub in 1885. There was a George Wickenden, possibly the husband, listed at No.2 Malta Cottages in 1867, and in George Street, in business as a carman, in 1868. Harriet Wickenden remained the licensee until 1876 or a little later.

The original pub of the 1860s was probably no bigger than the other Malta Cottages adjoining. Their scale can still be seen on the flank of the present building, because a damaged section of the wall had to be rendered when the cottage attached to the Gipsy Hill side was demolished. One newspaper report gives 1892 as the rebuilding date of the Railway Bell, and that is consistent with the style. The most enduring of the landlords in the existing pub have been Charles William Morgan, who was there for a dozen years at the beginning of the twentieth century, and Cecil John Paine, who was in charge from 1936-53. In recent decades the pub has achieved a reputation as one of the best in the district, and in 1981 Ron and Peg Bushnell won the Standard Pub of the Year award.

The second Railway Bell in 1995.

The Railway Castle, No.360 Norwood Road

Unless by anticipation, this beerhouse is unlikely to have been called the Railway Castle from the first, as it existed before the railway came to Lower Norwood in 1856. The building, which had long been a shop, was unoccupied in 1851. The first notice of it as a pub is in the 1855 directory, where Thomas Wood, who probably went on to higher things at the Horns, is listed as a beer retailer at No.2 Castle Place. Mrs Jane Bishop has the equivalent entry in the 1860 edition, and in the 1861 census Charles Mead, a twenty-seven-year-old beer shop keeper, heads the second household in Castle Place.

The Railway Castle name first appears during the seven years, from 1864-1871, when the pub was run by James Warren, a young man born in Norwood around 1838. It was an odd combination of two elements. Warren obviously wished to attract some railway trade, even though the station is 300 yards away. He was on firmer ground with the Castle, because the original name for this terrace of shops, as has already been seen, was Castle Place. No.2 later became No.200 Norwood Road, but it is now No.360. See the Knight's Hill Tavern (the beerhouse two doors away) for more about Castle Place. By 1872 the Railway Castle had closed and the building was empty. Within a few years it had been taken over by a plumber. The pub was a single-storey building, but the shop has now had a second floor added.

The Railway Tavern, No.34 Stroud Road

This pub might perhaps have justified its name on the grounds of being the nearest one to Woodside station, but it was not very close. It was beside the footbridge over the railway lines that give access to Addiscombe Road, but that path can hardly have brought many customers to the Railway Tavern. In fact, with the Beehive and the Joiner's Arms close by at Woodside Green it is hard to imagine where this third pub of the village picked up its trade. The three shops of Railway Terrace were built soon after 1868, and No.1 (the future pub) was used in the early years as a laundry. It was turned into a beerhouse in 1883 by James Dharty, who in the previous year had been living in Parchmore Road, Thornton Heath, while Drill Instructor to the Middlesex Yeomanry.

Several of the subsequent landlords stayed for a decade or more. Charles Frederick Baldry was there from 1887-97, and Charles Edward Gunnell from 1906-17. The Railway Tavern was certainly a beerhouse until then. The full licence seems to have been acquired by C.E. Randell, landlord from 1919 to the mid-1930s. The last lisencee was Mrs Jane Collis, who is listed at the Railway Tavern in 1939. She continued to live there after the war, but as a private resident. The former pub remained a house until at least the 1960s, but has now been the offices of Fox Preservatives Ltd for a number of years. It still looks entirely like a corner pub.

The Rambler's Rest, No.10 Hamlet Road

Mrs Jinks, who might be considered a rival, as her family ran the Windmill Tea Gardens in Westow Hill, produced this rather inaccurate memory of the Rambler's Rest in 1889:

> There was a wood down Anerley. The first house built there was a public house called the 'Rambler's Rest'. A man named Vivian lived there, but he was commonly known as 'Bungaroo'. The house stood near St Paul's Church, and I believe the very house is now occupied by a postman. He [Vivian] had a great many visitors on Sundays, and he made a very good thing out of it, ultimately selling it and buying some houses at Penge. He left Norwood before the Palace came.

Another impression was recorded in 1907 by W.C. Nicholls, who remembered that:

> at Hamlet Road was an old public house called the 'Ramblers' Rest', kept by a man who belonged to the Yeomanry, who always rode a beautiful grey horse; when the houses began to increase this inn was sold for £1,300.

Belvedere House in Belvedere Road is older than the pub, but it was certainly one of the first built in the Anerley wood, probably in 1851. There is no sign of it in the 1851 census, but in 1852 a directory lists 'John Ely Viviane, Royal Beulah Spa tea gardens, Hamlet Road'. The real Beulah Spa pleasure gardens in Beulah Hill were still open at that time, and Viviane was evidently trying to profit by the prestige of the name. In 1854 J.E. Vivian was rated for a house valued at £17 per annum, the present No.10 Hamlet Road, and for a cottage valued at £8, which was almost certainly the present No.12. As they were the only houses in Hamlet Road at the time there was ample room for the tea gardens. By 1855 the Crystal Palace had eclipsed the glory of the Beulah Spa and all other local rivals, so in that year the directory lists, 'John Ely Viviane, Rambler's Rest, Hamlet Road', the second and final name of the establishment.

The former Railway Castle and Knights Hill Tavern (the second and fourth shops from the corner of Lansdowne Hill) in 2000.

The former Railway Tavern in 2006.

Mrs Jinks was also wrong in saying that Vivianne left before the Crystal Palace came. He was still the landlord in 1860. By 1864 he had sold the pub to Thomas Barton, who is listed at the Rambler's Rest in that year. But in 1865 the directory lists Thomas Barton as a builder at this house, which by then was known as No.1 Hamlet Cottages. Development was now proceeding merrily in Anerley wood, and this must have been a convenient site for a builder's yard. The only surprise is that it was not replaced by a large villa when Barton no longer needed it for that purpose. Instead, Nos 10 and 12 survive anomalously as the only small houses in Hamlet Road.

The former Rambler's Rest in 2003, No.10
Hamlet Road in the centre, No.12 on the left.

THE RISING SUN, NO.72 ANERLEY ROAD

The Rising Sun in Anerley Road, which stood on the south-eastern corner of Anerley Vale, was founded in 1851 by William Nowell, a hatter from Southwark. He must only recently have moved to Norwood, because the 1851 census, in which he is described as a hatter, shows that his two-year-old daughter was born in Newington. This was before there was any question of the Crystal Palace coming to Norwood, so Nowell's cottage, almost certainly a new one, was isolated and lonely. Further up Anerley Hill there were a few large houses, but in the other direction almost nothing until Anerley Station. At the back was Anerley Wood, still undisturbed by building, and at the front the belt of trees that screened the park of Penge Place.

Nevertheless, in that same year of 1851 Nowell decided to turn his cottage into a beerhouse. An 1851 directory describes him as a beer seller etc., but whether the etc. involved hats or some other business cannot now be known. He needed a second string to his bow, as there was no local trade. The only customers for his beer must have been ramblers and other stray passers-by. Yet within two years this unpromising business became a gold-mine as Anerley Hill was overrun by swarms of thirsty navvies and builders working on the Crystal Palace site. With such a clientele the pub naturally became 'notorious as a noisy one', but Nowell managed nevertheless to obtain a full licence, and continued to milk the profits until 1860. By that time the Rising Sun had numerous local rivals and the golden years of the Crystal Palace boom were over.

One of his early successors, Walter Scott, in trying to improve the reputation of the pub by ejecting troublesome customers, found himself sued for assault in 1863. A witness reported that

Above: The Rising Sun, Anerley Hill, around 1870; with, further up the hill, glimpses of the Paxton Arms on the left, and the Brunswick on the right.

Left: Anerley Hill around 1950, showing the war damaged Rising Sun and Paxton Arms, the white buildings to left and right.

Opposite: The second Rising Sun, Spa Hill, c.1914. (John Gent)

one Francis Peters and his wife entered the pub and called for a pot of 'cooper', otherwise porter improved, which was served in a tankard:

> The female made some remark about being supplied with a glass. Mrs Scott made answer that not one person in twenty required a glass for drinking cooper. The Peters continued to make remarks and said that had they been dressed in their Sunday clothes they would have been served with a glass. He heard Peters say to Mrs Scott, 'You have got on a fine crinoline, what have you got under it?' Mrs Scott sent for her husband, who desired Peters and his wife to go out, and ejected them with some force.

Although Scott was acquitted, he remained at the Rising Sun for less than a year. The pub's attractions for its landlords did not increase with time; not one remained for as long as five years. The Rising Sun was damaged by bombing during the Second World War, and remained derelict for some years afterwards, before being demolished between 1952-1957. Flats and a mini-market are now on the site.

THE RISING SUN, NO.23 SPA HILL

The curious thing about the Rising Sun in Spa Hill is that there was a beer shop on the spot from the 1830s to 1853, but then only a private house until 1867. Whether the earlier pub was called the Rising Sun is unknown, but it was certainly in the same building, the larger part of a semi-detached pair. The cottages were perhaps built in a uniform style, with the southern one being enlarged when it became a beerhouse. The first landlord was probably Henry Gillingham, later of the Holly Bush and the White Lion, who was living here from 1833-37, although no sources then mention it as a pub. Successors certainly identified as beersellers here were Charles Wright from 1838-40, George Wortley in 1841-2, Samuel Self from 1842-47, and Aaron Roffey from 1847-53, when the beer shop closed. Roffey is described as a gardener in the 1851 census, which suggests that his beer selling was already just a sideline. The owner in those early days was William Pawson of the Beulah Spa, and it may have been the declining fortunes of the pleasure gardens that put the pub out of business.

Aaron Roffey continued to live here until the early 1860s, but as a private resident. When this and the neighbouring properties were auctioned in 1861, with Roffey listed as one of the tenants, they were described as, 'six brick-built and slated cottages, with forecourts and gardens', but with no mention of one of them being a beerhouse.

In 1867 Alfred Martin of the Rising Sun, beer & wine retailer, applied for a spirit licence, which was refused. He tried again in the following years with no better success, and by 1871 had retired defeated. His successors, Edmund Owen and many others, settled for the humbler status, and the Rising Sun continued to be a wine and beerhouse to an unusually late date, not obtaining a full licence until the 1960s. Between 1868-94 the pub was rebuilt in its present form, at first with its original semi-detached partner still clinging to the north side. Since the Second World War the cottage has been replaced by a single-storey extension to the pub. The most notable landlords of the Rising Sun were the Laytons – Henry Layton from 1882-09, Frederick James Layton from 1910 to the mid-1930s, and Mrs S.A. Layton until the Second World War at least. The Rising Sun fell on hard times after the war, and in 1965 ran out of beer because the bills had not been paid. The pub was rescued by Dennis Flannigan, landlord for a decade or so from 1965, who earned it the good reputation that it enjoys today.

The Rose & Crown, No.4 Crown Lane

The Rose & Crown is one of the oldest of the Norwood pubs, founded before the enclosure of the commons began the serious development of the area at the beginning of the nineteenth century. Until then there was only a scattered population living in a fringe of buildings on the edge of the commons, and nibbling away at them whenever the manorial authorities were looking the other way. The Rose & Crown stood at the extreme point of the Knights Hill tongue of enclosed land, which pushed up between the commons in Lambeth and Streatham until halted by the common in Croydon. John Rocque's 1740s map marks this area as Knights Hill Pound, and his 1762 map places Pound House on this corner. A pound was clearly needed in such a spot, where animals set to graze on one common were very apt to wander onto another. Neither map indicates a public house, buildings that Rocque was generally good at recording, so it is probable that the Rose & Crown was founded between 1762-84, when the first landlord

The second Rose & Crown, c.1905. (John Gent)

The third Rose & Crown in 2001.

can be identified. He was Thomas Boucher or Bowcher, who was licenced for the Rose & Crown from 1784-87.

Norwood was then becoming popular with day-trippers from London, and especially with artists, who came to sketch the scenery and the gypsies. Joseph Farington and John Hoppner dined at the Crown at Norwood in August 1798, and over their wine they talked about Reynolds's portrait of Lord Thurlow. It was a natural choice of topic, as Thurlow's controversial Knight's Hill House must then have been one of the most prominent landmarks visible from the pub.

The licensees in the early nineteenth century were presumably from the same family as the Thomas Boucher or Bowcher of the 1780s, but the name continued to give trouble. In 1803 it appeared as John Bourchier, in 1805 as Widow Boucher, and in 1807 as Isabella Bourchier. This last was probably correct, as in 1818 *The Times* carried an advertisement giving notice to Isabella Bourchier of the Rose & Crown, Norwood, about two hogsheads of potatoes that she had failed to collect from a ship. In the 1820s and early 1830s the landlord was George Nell. He was succeeded by the pub's celebrity, Edward Neale (1805-46), 'a pugilist well-known in his best days as the Streatham Youth'. Thomas Frost, the Croydon journalist, calls the fighter Ned O'Neale and gives an account of his Irish mother, an itinerant fish seller, but Neale is the name given in all the records. He began his career in 1822 and retired to Norwood in 1831, after being beaten twice by 'Young Dutch' Sam and once by Tom Gaynor. As the first fight against Young Dutch lasted for seventy-one rounds and that against Gaynor for forty-five it is perhaps hardly surprising that Edward Neale died at the age of forty-one. He is buried in boxer's corner at Norwood Cemetery. He left a widow Mary (his second wife of that name) who carried on the pub until 1854. A thirty-one-year lease was then offered for sale 'by the trustees of E. Neal, deceased'. The purchaser was George Bartlett, who remained until 1863. He was succeeded by William Neale, perhaps a son of the boxer, who was the landlord in 1864 and 1865.

The Rose & Crown seen in old photographs does not have an eighteenth-century appearance, as far as one can judge behind the advertising boards and ground floor additions, so it was presumably rebuilt in the nineteenth century. But as the style is not at all the flamboyant late Victorian one, the rebuilding is likely to have taken place in the 1850s or 1860s. The last landlords in this second Rose & Crown were Robert Thomas Godfrey (who sometimes appeared as Godfrey & Co.) from 1912-29, and William Maclaren (or Maclaren & Co.) from 1930-40. On 18 October 1940 the Rose & Crown received a direct hit that killed forty-eight people, including the landlord 'Mac' Maclaren. The pub was a free house before the war. It was eventually rebuilt by Watney Coombe Reid in 1956-57 as a tied house. When the brewers re-opened it in July 1957, the manager they appointed was Thomas Shepherd, a former chief inspector of police.

(The Rose & Crown had a beer shop satellite, name unknown, at Rose Cottage, between the pub and Knight's Hill. It was established in the 1840s, and run by John Cullum, who appears in various sources either as a carpenter or as a carpenter and beer retailer. He and his beerhouse are last heard of in 1865.)

The Rosemary Branch, No.79 Knights Hill

The first Rosemary Branch was not built as a pub, but spent some forty years as a private house, known in its later years as Tivoli Cottage after the nearby pleasure gardens. It was converted into a beerhouse in the late 1850s. The only significant change made then was the addition of the wing on the uphill side. The matching downhill wing was original. The occupant of the house between 1824 and the early 1830s was probably John Lyne, or Lynes, who continued to be the owner until at least the 1840s. Early in that decade his tenant was James Smith, a solicitor. We know that the rent of Tivoli Cottage was £20 per annum because the tenant (probably not James Smith by then) was bankrupt in 1847, and the lease was auctioned by the mortgagee. In 1851 Tivoli Cottage was occupied by Charles Dayle, a retired brush maker.

Between 1855-60 (possibly in 1858, when the lease expired) it was acquired by George Sparks, the founder of the pub. He probably called it the Rosemary Branch from the first, although the earliest mention I can find of the name is in 1867. It may have been an allusion to Sparks's other trade, for in 1872 he is described as 'George Sparks, beer retailer, nurseryman, seedsman, and florist'. There was plenty of ground for horticulture behind the pub. Later this was converted into 'Pleasure & Tea Gardens, Good Quoit Ground', as a notice on the front of the building expressed it. There was a surprisingly large area available for fun and games between Knight's Hill and the High Street, because the Rosemary Branch Tea Gardens ran back to the Tivoli Gardens attached to the King's Head.

George Sparks spent more than thirty years at the Rosemary Branch, setting up what was almost a country pub and staying until 1890, when the area was completely urbanised. But while Norwood was changing, the pub remained unaltered. It was not until 1896 that the Rosemary Branch was rebuilt to harmonise with its new environment. The process of urbanisation was underlined in 1912 when the bus garage was established at No.75 Knight's Hill, although Petty's old-established plumbing business at No.77 remained as a buffer between the garage and the pub until the 1920s. It was perhaps in the hope of attracting busmen that the brewers built a club room extension at the rear in 1913. The new Rosemary Branch was a mere beerhouse, like its predecessor, and continued so until at least the late 1950s. There was a slight concession to modernity in 1936 when the Jug and Bottle Dept was enlarged and renamed the Off Sales Dept.

The first Rosemary Branch, *c.*1890. (Lambeth Archives)

The bus garage that had been creeping up on it for so long finally destroyed the Rosemary Branch late in 1977 or early in 1978. London Transport had decided to rebuild the garage on a much larger scale, and the pub was one of the neighbouring properties acquired and demolished to realise this ambition.

THE ROSENDALE, NO.65 ROSENDALE ROAD

The Rosendale Hotel may have its origins in the very earliest days of the Thurlow Park Estate, where building began tentatively in the late 1840s. The 1851 census, among the scattered houses in these new roads, lists 'Joseph Potter, 36, conductor [?] of ale house, Rosendale, Park Road'. There is no record of any other drinking establishment in this area, and for some time after 1851 there would have been no call for more than one, as the population was small. The first definite mention of the pub comes in 1860, when Thomas Hugh Parnell is listed at the Rosendale Arms. A map published in 1862, but probably surveyed a year or two earlier, marks it as the Rosendale Hotel, and that is Parnell's address in the 1865 and 1867 directories. Most of the later landlords stayed only briefly. The main exceptions were George Frederick Payne, who was in charge from 1909-29, and Frank Farrell from 1932-49. When the pub was leased for forty years from 1885 the

Left: The Rosendale Hotel in 1913. (John Gent)

rent was £130 per annum, so the landlords needed to be doing good business if they were to make a profit. The Rosendale Hotel has the unique distinction among Norwood pubs of being Grade II Listed by English Heritage as a building of architectural importance.

THE ROYAL ALBERT, NO.42 WESTOW HILL

The Royal Albert is the only heir and successor to the Westow Hill windmill. In 1830 or soon after James Bakon (or Baken, or Baker) established a small beerhouse in front of the mill, probably in an existing cottage. It may possibly have been called the Crown & Anchor, or the Windmill. Early in 1853 it was taken over by one Thomas Nunn, who almost immediately demolished the beerhouse, acquired the whole mill property, and built a new and much larger pub, the parapet tastefully embellished with pineapples, on the Westow Hill frontage. The rateable value of the old beerhouse was £15, that of the new one £75, though it was only a two-storey building.

In the May 1853 rate book, the first to list the new pub, it is described as The Mill Beerhouse, which seems at first glance like a name. So it may have been temporarily, but as the words 'The Mill' are written larger than 'Beerhouse', it is likely that Nunn, having bought the mill, was rated originally for that only, and that the rest of the entry was added when he began to build his new pub. It may be worth noting that in 1839 it was claimed that, 'Londoners only know Norwood from the situation of the Woodman and the Windmill, where the Gypsies congregate'. If 'the Mill' or 'the Windmill' *was* the original name, it was very soon abandoned, for in August 1853 Thomas Nunn, 'of the Crystal Tower, Westow Hill', called a public meeting there to raise a subscription for the families of the workmen killed during the construction of the Crystal Palace. This was the scaffolding accident on 15 August in which thirteen died.

By April 1854 Nunn was trying to sell a long lease 'of the Royal Albert and Crystal Tower Tavern'. He had presumably despaired of obtaining a full licence in an area already so well supplied with inns, for in his advertisement, after boasting of the 'immense cost of erection', he claimed that 'it is reduced to almost a certainty that a licence for the sale of wines and spirits will be granted at the next licensing day'. The member of the inexhaustible army of suckers who rose to the bait was James John Edward Pool, who was listed in 1855 at the Royal Albert and Crystal Tower Hotel. But he quickly realised his mistake, and offloaded the beerhouse to John Cooley. It was Cooley who had full leisure to appreciate the beauty of Thomas Nunn's joke, as he spent the next thirty years in vain pursuit of that 'almost certain' full licence. Nunn had even found means to improve his jest by setting up a rival in Cooley's back yard. In the rear part of the property he had allowed the establishment (or revival) of the Windmill Tea Gardens, cutting off one of the expedients by which Cooley might have compensated himself for his failure to obtain that licence.

But Cooley was clearly an enterprising man, and he found other ways of raising his pub above the level of ordinary beerhouses. He streamlined the name to the now familiar Royal Albert, and he built or acquired extensive stabling (much needed in the early days of the Crystal Palace) so that in the late 1850s this upstart beerhouse had a higher rateable value than the nearby Woodman, one of the premier inns of Norwood. He took in lodgers: eight are listed in the 1871 census. Above all, like many a modern publican, he stressed the catering side of the business, calling his house 'the Royal Albert chop and dining rooms'.

John Cooley finally left the pub in 1884, and within five years one of his early successors, Walter Henry Meadows, had worked part of the trick that had defeated Cooley for so long by obtaining a wine licence. For spirits, though, the wait still continued. If Wilson is correct in saying that the Royal Albert was rebuilt in its present form just before the Second World War, then the next landlord to make a real mark on the history of the pub was T.W. Harper, who was in charge during the late 1930s.

There are several odd points about this rebuilding. The original Royal Albert was on the same building line as the shops on either side. Why should the owner want his new pub set back so far from the street, sacrificing valuable bar space? And supposing that for some reason he did, what

Part of the first Royal Albert, c.1914.

The second
Royal Albert
in 1998.

would make the council allow it, when they were normally such sticklers for maintaining the building line? And why is the present Royal Albert built like a semi-detached property, with the eastern flank wall seeming to be waiting patiently for another half that is never built? The only explanation I can suggest is that there was an aspiration to gradually rebuild the whole south side of Westow Hill on this new line, so as to widen the road. The most notable personality at the new pub has been the 1950s landlord Leonard David Cowan, who was described by Laurie Cudby of the Upper Norwood library as 'Dave Cowan of the Albert with his polished manner and gorgeous waistcoats'.

THE ROYAL CRYSTAL PALACE HOTEL, NOW THE PALACE, NO.2 ANERLEY HILL

The only rival to the Queen's for the title of Norwood's leading hotel has had an eventful, and on the whole not a very successful career. It was built in 1853, as the Crystal Palace rose majestically just across the road, to designs by the firm of Wehnert & Ashdown. The projector of the new hotel, the magnificently extravagant Thomas Masters, had bought and demolished Mantua House, a boarding school that advertised 'education in a superior ladies' establishment, uniting all the advantages of a ladies' collegiate school with the refinements of an elegant house'. The news of the impending arrival of the palace had caused a property boom all over the district. This commanding corner plot was of unrivalled quality in these new circumstances, and its sale, even if it was only of the lease, must have provided a wonderful profit for the three young sisters, Mary, Sarah and Elizabeth Elliott, who ran the school.

In October 1854 there were advertisements for the Royal Crystal Palace Hotel, Thomas Masters sole proprietor, with upwards of one hundred rooms, plus, 'a private mansion, adjoining the grounds of the above hotel, suitable for first-class families'. Could this have been Cintra in Church Road? It was the only mansion adjoining the hotel, but in an advertisement 'a man is not upon oath', Masters may have been referring grandiloquently to the Church Road wing of the hotel, now the only original part surviving.

Not content with this enormous establishment, and filled with enthusiastic belief in the pulling power of the Crystal Palace, Masters had been buying pubs and hotels all over Upper Norwood. By 1855 he was not surprisingly bankrupt. In the next year the assignees and mortgagees of the Royal Crystal Palace Hotel & Tavern auctioned the furniture and fittings, which included 'handsome colossal figures', very much the sort of thing that Masters dealt in. They were offering:

> a lease of upwards of 90 years at the almost nominal rent of £225 per annum; also the stabling premises and stabling in the rear; also 1 and 2 Palace-terrace adjoining (shops with residences adjoining), let on lease to two respectable tenants at £160 per annum; also 3 and 4, not quite finished, with immediate possession.

Palace Terrace was presumably the Church Road wing. If so, the tenants of Nos 1 and 2 must have been disposed of, as the wing was rapidly reunited with the rest of the hotel.

The lease was taken by a limited company, known variously as the Crystal Palace Hotel Co., Master's Royal Crystal Palace Hotel Co. Ltd, and the Crystal Palace Royal Family Hotel Co. Ltd. There was a rapid succession of managers, none presumably very successful, and one a disaster. In 1864 a guest sued the company for assault after being turfed out of his bed in the middle of the night. He would only agree to settle the case, 'if an apology was made, the manager was dismissed, and the sum of one hundred guineas paid over to a charity to be named by him'. The company continued to run the hotel, rather less melodramatically, until the end of the nineteenth century,

The Royal Crystal Palace Hotel and the Cambridge Hotel, c.1910. (Upper Norwood Joint Library)

The boarded-up Sportsman (successor to the Royal Crystal Palace Hotel) in 1998.

when Corbet Anderson noted that 'there has just been added to it a handsome billiard room, containing four fine billiard tables'.

Edwin Henry Gilbert bought the hotel for £5,500 in October 1918, and was the landlord until his death. In 1935 his executors sold it to William Younger & Co., the Scottish brewers, who made no secret of their intention to rebuild the pub on a smaller scale and exploit the development potential of the rest of the site. The Second World War halted their plans, but then seemed to co-operate with them when the greater part of the building was demolished by a bomb. The Anerley Hill frontage was entirely destroyed. The Church Road wing and the ballroom at the rear survived, and a temporary bar in the ballroom kept the business going until the present Anerley Hill buildings (presumably cobbled together from the surviving materials of the old hotel) were ready in 1956. At that point, in humble recognition of reduced circumstances, the pub was renamed the Crystal Palace Inn.

Younger's had not forgotten their plans for the site, and as soon as post-war austerity allowed they were brought forward again. A proposal to demolish the Crystal Palace Inn and replace it with a nine-storey office block, with a pub on the ground floor, was in discussion from 1962-73, at least. A clash of opinions and contradictory planning decisions issued by three authorities, Penge Urban District Council, Kent County Council, and Bromley Council, delayed things for so long that the brewers despaired, though in the early 1980s they did compensate themselves for the disappointment by selling the old ballroom at the rear to be part of Smith's garage, now demolished. The last two decades have been chiefly marked by changes of name. The pub was the Sportsman from 1982 or 1983 to 1998. It re-opened as The Occasional Half in May 1999 after major alterations, including the addition of two porches, but this name survived only until 2003. Then, happily, the pub returned closer to tradition when it became the Palace, or Jack Beard's at the Palace.

THE ROYAL OAK, BEULAH HILL

This little beerhouse was demolished before the numbering of Beulah Hill was settled, but its site is now occupied by No.54, the magnificent St Valery. The Royal Oak lasted for no more than twenty-five years as a pub, and even the building stood for less than fifty years, during nearly all of which it was occupied by one family. It is first heard of in 1834, when Edward Howard was rated for a 'cottage and improvement'. By 1836 he was listed as a 'retailer of beer'. He may have died between then and 1839, when Mrs Mary Howard had become the landlady. The Royal Oak name is first recorded in 1838, and was no doubt used from the first. Mrs Howard added a second string to her bow, as she is listed in 1845 as a grocery dealer, and in 1852 as a grocer and beer retailer. In his *Notes on Norwood*, referring to the 1850s, Rupert Montague Browne calls it 'Mrs Howard's sweet and bacon shop standing solitary'. As there was also a blacksmith's forge in the yard, the Royal Oak was a complete service station for the Victorian traveller.

At this period Mrs Howard apparently had some difficulties with her landlord, the Archbishop of Canterbury, perhaps about a renewal of the lease, which resulted in the archbishop being briefly rated as the keeper of a beerhouse. These problems were resolved, and Mary Howard makes a final appearance in an 1855 directory as 'beer retailer, Beulah road, Upper Norwood'. In the rate books, however, she is last listed in May 1854. She was about seventy by then, and must have died or retired soon after. That seems to have been the end of the beerhouse.

Elizabeth Dee remembered that when she walked along Beulah Hill with her husband in 1858, 'some little distance past Harold Road we came to a very quaint shop, where almost anything you wanted was sold; it had a lot of outbuildings, and was occupied by Mr Howard the Norwood Carrier'.

Directories suggest that the business was split, with William Howard running the grocery and provision shop, and John Howard acting as the carrier. Carriers were important local figures, handling the parcel post of their district to and from London, until modern transport methods enabled national companies to monopolise that work. Benjamin Howard took over from John, and continued to act as the Upper Norwood carrier from the yard behind the shop until at least 1874. In the 1870s the grocery business was taken over by William Pringle. By that time the Ecclesiastical Commissioners, as successors to the Archbishop of Canterbury, were keen to make more profitable use of this valuable land. Howard and Pringle jumped, or were pushed, and St Valery was built on the site around 1880.

THE ROYAL STANDARD, GIPSY HILL

This was the address given in *The Times* in November 1856 by a potman and ostler seeking a place. It could possibly have been the earlier name of the second George IV.

THE SHAFTSBURY, NO.41 ST GOTHARD ROAD

This building at the corner of St Cloud Road, now used for housing, bears a plaque reading 'Shaftesbury Terrace 1879', presumably the building date, and a corner sign that says 'The Shaftesbury, full off-licence, Lacons'. After serving briefly as a grocer's and fishmonger's shop in the early 1880s, the building seems to have been an off-licence during most of that decade. John Mulley is listed there as a wine & spirit and beer retailer in 1884 and as a wine & spirit merchant in 1886.

Above left: The former Shaftesbury in 2003.

Above right: The Ship in 1998.

But from 1890 the listing for Francis A. Dickenson and his successors is consistently 'beer retailer', which usually means a beerhouse. In the 1891 census he appears as, 'Frederick Dickenson, 35, beer retailer, Off-Licenced Public House, 217 Rommany Road', which I take to mean a pub with an off-licence attached.

From the 1950s the business was owned by companies, Ward Houses Ltd, and Thresher & Co., both still described as beer retailers, though Thresher's is certainly an off-licence chain. The last trace of the Shaftesbury before it closed was in 1970, when it was run by D.M. Worrall, wine & spirit merchant. This building, then, probably began, and certainly ended its connection with the drink trade as an off-licence, but perhaps had a spell as a beerhouse in between. The street pattern here has been seriously disturbed since the 1970s by the building of council estates, and this detached part of the old Rommany Road has been renumbered in St Gothard Road.

THE SHIP, NO.55 SOUTH NORWOOD HIGH STREET

It is curious that the two South Norwood pubs popularly supposed to have a connection with the Croydon Canal – one correctly, one probably not – should have such inappropriate names. Why the Ship and the Jolly Sailor, when the Barge and the Jolly Bargeman would have been so much more suitable? That the Jolly Sailor was named in allusion to the canal workers seems certain nevertheless, but the Ship is a far less conclusive case.

The skittle alley of the Ship in 1912. (John Gent)

A building on the site was contemporary with the canal, and stood next to one of the access paths to its Norwood Wharf. This was almost certainly the route along which the bricks from Pascall's pottery on the other side of the High Street were carried to the waiting barges. But the building on the Ship site was not then a pub, and was not directly connected with the canal, though the horses that dragged the barges probably came to know it well. The predecessor of the Ship was a blacksmith's forge, run by George Baker in the 1820s and early 1830s, by William Gourd in the years around 1840, and by George Baker again (perhaps the son) in the early 1850s.

The forge continued in business after Daniel Lancaster built the Ship in 1852, but its rateable value was reduced by more than half, from £7 to £3, indicating that a large part of the property had been taken over by the new pub. The rateable value of the Ship was £30 during the 1850s. Although Daniel Lancaster was the creator of the pub, he was not quite the first landlord. One George Webb is listed as his tenant in 1852. But Lancaster took charge himself in 1853, and remained for ten years, obtaining the coveted full licence in 1857.

In 1863 Lancaster applied to transfer the licence to Mrs Charlotte Westwood, a widow. The dubious bench was told that some of the best inns in the country were kept by widows. Mrs Westwood had little chance to prove her worth, as she was dead within two years. Few of the later licensees stayed for long. The exception was Frederick James Bye, who served from 1914-28, and was briefly succeeded by Mrs E.E. Bye. Before 1914 the pub had a successful skittles team, known as the Ship Hotel Timber Club, that wiped the floor with opponents from as far away as Catford, Sydenham and Herne Hill. It is the most attractive of the High Street pubs, and continues to be popular.

Left: The former Sidney Arms in 1998.

Opposite: The Signal Hotel in 1953. (Croydon Local Studies Library)

THE SIDNEY ARMS, NO.1 SIDNEY ROAD

The little back-street corner pub is becoming as rare as the corner shop. Most of the Norwood examples have disappeared as a result of slum clearance or redevelopment, but here is one that survives, though used now as a private house. The Sidney Arms was founded as a beerhouse, probably in 1879, by Richard Winter, a former carpenter who had come from the Joiner's Arms at Woodside Green. He remained until 1886. In his day the corner position caused some confusion to directory publishers, who listed the pub in Carmichael as often as in Sidney Road. The longest serving of Winter's successors was Walter Padbury, who was the landlord for thirty years from 1893-1922. The Sidney Arms continued as a beerhouse at least until 1939, when L.J. Stephenson was the publican, but it closed either during the war or just after, for by the early 1950s it was an off-licence. One curious point is that the business (whether pub or off-licence) was run by Ernest W. and Evelyn M. Taylor in the 1940s, and by Ernest W. and Evelyn M. Saunders in the 1950s, which seems too great a coincidence. The old pub was converted into a house in the 1960s.

THE SIGNAL HOTEL, NOW THE PORTMANOR, PORTLAND ROAD

This prominent pub was known briefly as the Railway Signal, then as the Signal Hotel for one hundred and twenty-five years until it became the Portmanor. The original name was chosen because the Jolly Sailor station was almost next door. But within a few years of opening the founders of the pub had the disappointment of seeing the new Norwood Junction, much further away, replace the first station. It was then, in 1859, that the word 'Railway' was dropped from the name. The owners, the brewers Nalder & Co., put in Thomas Miller as the first landlord, in

1855, but he was almost immediately replaced by Mrs Alice Miller. The Railway Signal was a beerhouse then, but Alice Miller obtained a full licence at her second attempt, in 1857.

The most noteworthy of the later licensees were Edward and Anne E. Barnett, who ran the pub in succession from 1904 until the Second World War. The pub had to endure hard times in the early 1980s, with a mysterious fire and a prolonged closure, but after a considerable enlargement it reopened as the Portmanor in 1985. There is a distinct touch of class about its having no street number. The pub was 'the Railway Signal, near the Station' in the early days, and is now just the 'Portmanor, Portland Road'.

THE SOUTH NORWOOD BREWERY TAP, No.14 ALBERT ROAD

The South Norwood Brewery was a notably unsuccessful venture, and its Tap fared even worse. The brewery lasted only from 1865-70, but in that brief career had at least three proprietors, Sidney Johnson from 1865-67, Inge and Cocks in 1868, and Maurice Gravett in 1869. In 1866 the brewery was sold 'together with a valuable public house site', and in 1868 Richard Lewis, beer retailer, is listed next door. He is the only known landlord. When another attempt (apparently unsuccessful) was made to sell the brewery in 1870, the property included a 'brick-built and slated Detached Dwelling House, recently used as a Brewery Tap'. That is the last that is heard of the brewery or the pub as a going concern. The site remained vacant for a decade before the old brewery became Keen's Empress Bicycle Works in 1879 or 1880. It was later a builder's yard.

As far as I can tell the old Tap became No.14 Albert Road, used at one time as a private residence and at another occupied by a gasfitter. It survived the Second World War, but the whole area was cleared afterwards to make way for the new St Mark's School.

THE SOUTH NORWOOD RAILWAY HOTEL, NOW THE CHERRY TREE, NO.32 STATION ROAD

When the Signal Hotel was so unfortunate as to be deserted by the station in 1859 the South Norwood Railway Hotel was one of several that sought to profit by its misfortune. But Norwood Junction was built in the middle of a field, and eager pub speculators had to wait until Station Road and Clifford Road (originally Lower Station Road) were laid out in the early 1860s before the building race could begin. The first application for a licence for the Railway Hotel was made in March 1865 by Thomas Linton Priddle, a builder who told the bench that he had retired to run this house and spent £3,000 on it; the furnishing was not yet complete. A licence was refused as the magistrates thought a pub was not needed here 'at present', even though the station had been open for five or six years. The pub operated as a beerhouse for the time being. Priddle quickly lost interest, and let it to one John Jarman, who obtained a full licence at his second attempt in 1867.

The Railway Hotel suffered a setback in 1871 when, despite protests from Jarman, the Norwood Junction refreshment room got a full licence. It was perhaps this that prompted him to hand over in that year to 'William Bishop, late of Catherine Street, Strand'. But in general the pub was prosperous. The most notable landlord was George William Amer, formerly at the Clifton Arms, who was in charge from 1886-1906. From 1909 the licence was held by Mrs Jane

The South Norwood Railway Hotel, c.1905. (John Gent)

Bigmore Westall, who soon became Mrs Jane Bigmore Frary. The Frary family continued to run the Railway Hotel until the Second World War. It is natural to suppose that bomb damage led to the removal of the second storey, giving the pub its present ugly, truncated appearance, but there is no record of a bomb falling here. Perhaps, as at the White Swan, it was a case of post-war economy. Another major change followed around 1980, when the new name appeared. Early reports said that the Cherry Trees was the choice, but it is now the Cherry Tree.

THE SPREAD EAGLE NOW THE GOLD COAST, NO.224 PORTLAND ROAD

The Spread Eagle was one of a group of pubs built in the mid-1860s when the development of the Enmore Park estate opened up this agricultural area (See the Gladstone for more details). It was probably built in 1866, as a licence was refused to the Eagle Tavern, South Portland Road in March 1867. The landlady in 1868 was Mrs Sarah Banks, who is listed as a beer retailer. She in her turn failed to obtain a full licence in that year. In 1870 Joseph Bedwell and Charles Thomas Ball, when trying unsuccessfully again, said 'the house was situated in a populous area; the Chairman remarked that there was a perfectly open country beyond it'. John Pinn, who was landlord from 1875-96, tried again, and was refused again, in 1876. He did obtain a wine licence, and settled temporarily for being a wine & beer retailer. The coveted full licence was not achieved until the 1880s. The Spread Eagle has had several long-serving landlords. Just two, Frederick George Pike and Percy Fitchett, were in charge from the Boer War to the Second World War. It was still the Spread Eagle at least until the late 1980s, but since then it has been called the Pheasant in the late 1990s, and now the Gold Coast.

The Spread Eagle in 1960. (Croydon Local Studies Library)

THE STAR HOTEL, NO.18 ANERLEY HILL

The Star Hotel was built between 1851-54. The peculiar, top-heavy appearance of the building may suggest that it was begun as a two-storey private house, but was extended upwards when the builders heard the great news about the Crystal Palace in 1853. In 1854 it was occupied by William Wade Westbrook, who in the next year is listed as running a coffee and chop house. He obtained a licence in 1856, but was soon in trouble with the bench for harbouring thieves. He managed to talk himself out of it, telling the magistrates that 'the hotel was fitted up suitable for families of the highest distinction, and was worth thousands of pounds.' The name 'the Star Hotel' is first recorded in 1860. Westbrook applied to transfer the licence to his widowed mother in 1866. The dubious magistrates were assured by the police that the Star did 'mostly hotel business, a very quiet house indeed'. Mrs Eliza Westbrooke was in charge, at least nominally, until 1872.

Thereafter the hotel had a troubled history, being closed as often as it was open. In 1880 one Penniston Dunn tried the modern idea of changing the name, to the Star & Garter Hotel, in the hope of a change of fortune, but the device was no more successful then than it is today. In 1887 the furniture, stock-in-trade, and effects came under the hammer, and when the dust settled the Star & Garter Hotel emerged as Cintra House, the private residence of Henry Thomas Silverlock. The forty-nine-year unexpired lease was sold for £500 in 1901, at which time Silverlock was paying an annual rent of £100 and a ground rent of £43.

By 1903 the building had been converted again, this time into a boarding house. It was run by a man whose extraordinary name gave predictable trouble to directory compilers. He appears as Yakoof Preelooker in 1903, and as Jacolf Prelooker in 1908. The building was empty again at the beginning of the First World War, just in time to provide a refuge for the Crystal Palace School of Practical Engineering, which had been evicted from the Palace by the Navy. The School remained at the old Star Hotel until 1930, when it moved to Harefield House, No.14 Anerley Hill. In the late

The former Star Hotel in 2003.

The Thurlow Arms in 1906. (John Gent)

1930s the old Star became the Cintra House Private Hotel (or boarding house), which was run by Mrs G. Eminton. By the early 1980s it was being used by Bromley Council as accommodation for homeless families, but in 1983 it was sold to a private developer. It is now divided into flats.

THE THURLOW ARMS, NO.551 NORWOOD ROAD

The Thurlow Arms, one of Norwood's leading inns, has been closed for some time and its future looks very uncertain. It was founded between 1846-50, and was one of the first buildings on the Thurlow Park estate, then just being opened up for development. The earliest licensee I can name is a Mrs Dangerfield, who was there in May 1850. Could she have been connected with Edward Dangerfield of Gipsy Hill, possibly an architect, who was landlord of the Masons' Arms? It is not a common name. By 1851 Mrs Dangerfield had been replaced by Mrs Ann Gardner, who was in charge until 1868. None of the other Victorian licensees remained for more than five years. Long-serving landlords in the twentieth century were Edward Robert Auckland from 1904-1930, and various members of the Beard family from 1942 until at least 1958.

The last decade has been eventful and unfortunate for the old pub. After a long closure it reopened at the beginning of 1998 as G.E. Aldwinckle's. By January 2000 it had become part of the Jack Stamp's chain, but that venture did not prosper, and the pub was closed and boarded up again by 2004. This handsome building, with its forecourt, is a key element of the townscape at the heart of West Norwood, so its loss would be a serious one.

LOS TOREROS, NO.35 WESTOW STREET

It is dubious whether this should be included, as it is more like a wine bar or licenced restaurant than a pub, but because of its close connection with the Postal Order I have allowed it in. The building was formerly the post office, when No.33 (now The Postal Order) was the sorting office. The post office closed in 1988 or 1989, and the building was vacant for about five years before being converted into a bar and restaurant. It was known as Rockwell's from 1998 or a little earlier, but became Los Toreros Tapas Bar around 2001. It is seen, as Rockwell's, in the photograph of the Postal Order on p.76.

The saloon bar of the Thurlow Arms, c.1910.

THE TULSE HILL HOTEL, No.150 NORWOOD ROAD

The original building on the Tulse Hill Hotel site was one of the lodges of the Tulse Hill estate. As such it is unlikely to have been built before 1820, when that development began. It was certainly there by 1824, as it appears on a map of that date, and it probably existed by October 1822, when *The Times*, in its list of 'partnerships dissolved' included 'J. Briscoe & R. Cripps, Tulse Hill, Surrey, nurserymen'. In 1823 there was an advertisement for a house in Tulse Hill, 'being the second house from the Lodge on the Norwood Road, particulars at the Lodge'. In the dissolution of the Briscoe-Cripps partnership it was Briscoe who departed, for in 1824 Richard Cripps was rated for a lodge and two acres of land, and in an 1826 directory he appears as 'Richard Cripps, nursery, seedsman, and florist'. In 1829 he was rated for lodge, land and improvements, and assessed on a £40 rateable value, an increase of £16 since 1824. Had his improvements involved rebuilding the house, and if so was the house he built the one that stands today? Probably not. Richard Cripps ran the nursery business until 1831.

In 1832 a directory lists John Jolly, nursery and seedsman, Norwood. This is the first appearance of Cripps's successor, although in later references he usually appears as William Jolley. Possibly there was a father and son. 'Mr Jolley's nursery, Tulse Hill, Norwood' is given as a servant's address in 1833, and in 1835 there was an advertisement for a display of grapes at Mr Jolly's nursery grounds. By 1840 William Jolly was rated for a house and garden ground with an annual value of £58, another substantial increase. That is the year in which Wilson claims the Tulse Hill Hotel was built, but he cites no evidence. William Jolley was still running the nursery in 1843, but it was not to last much longer.

The date at which the nursery was converted into an hotel can be established with some accuracy by reference to two advertisements. In December 1845 a landowner vainly promoting the idea of a pub in the Thomas's Place area of Norwood Road claimed that 'there is no public house on either of the roads from London within a mile'. The two roads from London were obviously Norwood Road and Tulse Hill, so unless the advertiser was lying outrageously Jolley's nursery must still have occupied the fork of those two roads. But in August 1847 an advertisement for some houses in Thurlow Place, Norwood Road, described them as being 'a short distance past the Tulse Hill Hotel'. We can say almost certainly, then, that the hotel was founded in 1846 or early in 1847. That is another plausible date for the building of the current house, and more likely than the late 1820s or 1840. That the new hotel sprang immediately into prominence is suggested by a sale of furniture that took place in January 1848, 'in the large assembly room, Tulse Hill Hotel'.

The earliest landlord I can name is William Crow, who was there in a rate book for September 1850 and in the 1851 census, aged fifty-nine. When a forty-year lease of the 'Tulse Hill Tavern, a cheerful roadside public house', was offered for sale in 1858 the advertisement noted that it had 'the advantage of the almost entire absence of effective competition'.

None of Crow's successors stayed for very long until the twentieth century, when the Burtwell family ran the pub for more than fifty years: Augustus Frederick Burtwell from 1907-30, his widow Emily from 1930-32, and his son George Augustus Burtwell from 1932 until he retired to Hove in 1961. It was Augustus Burtwell who built the rear extension as a lounge bar and billiard room. The wing to the north is much older, already in existence by 1870. By kind permission of George Burtwell's daughter, Mrs Jill Farmer, I am able to include her account of the building and staff in the 1940s:

The Tulse Hill Hotel, c.1870. (Lambeth Archives)

Augustus Frederick Burtwell, landlord of the Tulse Hill Hotel from 1907 to 1930. (Jill Farmer)

The staff were: Mrs Hannah Mary Betts, cook; Mr George Hollage, general handyman; his wife, assistant to cook; Miss Ethel Barratt, manageress and housekeeper; various cellarmen; Amy, helper to Mrs Hollage in the kitchen; two maids who worked for my mother in the house and served in the bars; our nanny; Jimmy who opened car doors and helped in the garage, and collected glasses from tables in the garden. There were three bars: the lovely lounge bar with doors that opened onto the garden, where there were many tables and chairs; a small private bar; and a large public bar with a coke fire. Underneath the bars were one very large cellar with a lift up to the public bar for crates of beer; a wine cellar, always locked; a coal cellar used by the family in the war as a shelter. Above the bars were our lounge (large enough for our grand piano), the family dining room, two bedrooms, two bathrooms, and our nursery. Above that a double bedroom for the maids, single bedroom for Miss Barratt, single bedroom for Mrs Betts, single bedroom for the cellarman, large bedroom for my grandmother. Although it was called a hotel, we were non-residential. The garden had many fruit trees including fig, mulberry, apple, pear, damson, and Victoria plum. A lovely fish pond with many goldfish and a fountain. My grandfather had a bowling green with a summer house fitted with shelves for the wooden bowls. Down the side of the garden were many lime trees, and outside the private front door a small garden with a lilac tree. All these were taken down when the road was widened.

The Tulse Hill Hotel is still in business, in what is probably the oldest pub building in Norwood, and certainly the most attractive.

THE TWO TOWERS, NO.201 GIPSY ROAD

The eagle-eyed will spot that this pub does not possess even one tower, merely two garden urns on plinths. The name is supposed to have been taken from the towers of the Crystal Palace, which loomed above the roof of the pub in happier days. The urns were perhaps added as some slight justification of the name after the original allusion had lost its point with the destruction of the Palace. The pub, which remained a mere beerhouse until the middle of the twentieth century, was founded by Joseph Moss in 1868 or a little earlier. The Two Towers is notable for the remarkably few landlords who ran it during its first century. Moss was succeeded in the 1880s by his widow Mary Ann, who remained until the mid-1890s. Frank Ellis held the licence from 1896-1912, when Miss Emily Letitia Ledger began an extraordinarily long reign that was unbroken in 1958. From 1956 she was in partnership with Jocelyn Hayes Power.

THE VICTORIA ARMS, NO.17 COVENTRY ROAD

This little beerhouse was not named directly in honour of the great queen, but after Victoria Road, the name for Coventry Road until 1913. The pub was opened in 1853 by Thomas Vinton. He was the owner as well as the landlord, which makes it likely that he was the builder or developer. If so, he followed the usual practice by quickly transferring the licence – to Ann Mann in 1856.

The Two Towers
in 1995.

The Victoria Arms, *c.* 1950. (Croydon Local Studies Library)

She did not stay long, but several of her successors seem to have been very devoted to the Victoria Arms. Edward Maxwell, who was there from 1859-74, tried several times to obtain a full licence. At his third or fourth attempt, in 1870, he sent his wife to represent him, saying he was ill, but the magistrates were not softened. Walter Frederick Athey was landlord from 1875-05, and George Alfred Milton from 1913 until at least 1958, an extraordinary length of service. The Victoria Arms was better known to its regulars as the Rat, on account of unwelcome visitors from Coldrey's bakery next door. The local rats could not kill the pub, but local politicians could when they decided to redevelop the area in the 1970s. The pub was demolished in 1973, and the site is now part of the playground of St Mark's school.

THE VICTORIA HOTEL, NO.99 CENTRAL HILL

The Victoria Hotel began as an unsuccessful speculation of pre-Crystal Palace Norwood, which was revived in 1853 when the news that the Palace was on its way created a sudden building boom. The projectors had left it as a carcase, the mere walls and roof of an intended private house, and as such it became a favourite adventure playground for the first generation of New Town children. In 1853 the carcase was snapped up by Thomas Masters of the Royal Crystal Palace Hotel, a great speculator in pubs in the early days of the Crystal Palace. He was rated for a beerhouse here, with a valuation of £60, in May 1853. By May of 1855 Masters had let it to Henry J. Bond, who was listed at The Lion Inn, valued at £100.

For the rest of the decade the owner was too busy with bankruptcy hearings to have much time for this minor piece of property, and Bond was left in quiet possession, but in 1859 Masters tried to sell it, advertising the pub as 'admirably calculated for conversion into a first-class private family hotel; it has hitherto been conducted as a tavern'. There were no bidders, so in 1860 Masters decided to take over the Lion himself. His attempts to evict Henry Bond resulted in rancorous legal disputes, but Masters quickly got his way. He immediately changed the name to the Victoria Hotel. The running of it was left to Mrs Masters, as her husband had many other irons in the fire. The attractions advertised were 'Spacious garden and good attendance. Foreign languages spoken. Good stabling and lock-up coach-houses.' To judge from the account of her dispute with a guest over the use of a pianoforte, Mrs Masters was somewhat of the Sybil Fawlty school of hotel management. Her ill temper was perhaps a reflection of the financial troubles she was facing, for in 1865 the Croydon magistrates were told, when deciding whether to grant a licence to the Oxford Arms, that in the Central Hill area there was 'not sufficient trade or traffic to make the Victoria Hotel answer'.

It closed in that year and remained empty for the rest of the decade. When a tenant was found in 1870 the building was not reopened as a pub or hotel, but became Victoria House, a reformatory for female servants run by the Society for the Rescue of Young Women. There were thirty-seven of these unfortunates at Victoria House in 1871. Under various dismal names this dismal institution, of which Mrs Merry was one long-serving matron, survived until the early 1930s. The old hotel was then converted into flats, and so it remains.

The former Victoria Hotel in 1995.

The White Hart, No.96 Church Road

The site of the White Hart was auctioned as 'valuable freehold building ground' in 1819. The pub was built in 1823-4, and known as the White Hart Inn by 1825, when an inquest was held there. It was first occupied by William Fox, presumably a member of the prominent local farming family that gave its name to Fox Hill. If so, this diversification proved unfortunate, for in 1835 the newspapers advertised 'the White Hart, with small tea garden and plot of building ground in front to be sold by consent of the mortgagee of W. Fox, a bankrupt'. Fox had been extravagant, especially in the case of his detached tea garden, an expensive luxury in an area of rising property prices. It was opposite the pub, in the triangle enclosed by Church Road, Lansdowne Place, and Fox Hill. William Farmer's reminiscences give a good picture of the old pub, except that it had two storeys, not one as he says:

> The White Hart was a wooden structure, one storey high, with trees and chains and posts in front. Under the trees were seats and tables, quite a country-looking inn, with the wayfarers refreshing in front, while pails of water and crates of hay were ready for the beasts.

The White Hart tea garden had:

> an entrance through the jaws of a whale, arbours all round, and a bowling green in the centre. Hither came many festive parties, and waiters from the White Hart ran busily to and fro with tea and other refreshments.

There was also a well in the tea garden, from which water was sold to the neighbourhood by the pail.

The Crystal Palace was the tea garden to end all tea gardens, and in Norwood it did put an end to them all during the 1850s. The dominant figure in the history of the White Hart is John Ledger, who was landlord from 1845 (when he was twenty-three or twenty-four) until 1878. For a hard-nosed businessman like Ledger, whose tea garden was only a sideline, this problem was easily turned into an opportunity. He began to build shops and houses on the site of the bowling green and arbours, and was soon making as much from rents as he ever had from the sale of tea and ices. There was no vestige of the tea gardens remaining by 1868. We get a brief glimpse of Ledger's personality from the bookseller William Farmer's account of taking a lease of one of his new shops in 1858. 'He did not appear much impressed with the idea of a library and booksellers, but expressed a strong opinion that a good ham & beef shop would answer.' Having got rid of the tea gardens, Ledger's final contribution was to get rid of the old inn as well, and replace it in 1876 or shortly before with the building we know today. The design is attributed to the Scottish architect, Sextus Dyball.

The new White Hart has had a number of long-serving landlords: David Jones 1886-96, Walter Edmund Everard 1898-1914, Thomas May from 1916-27, and Ken French from the late 1950s to the 1970s. The name was changed to O'Neill's in the late 1990s, when the pub was decorated in mock-Irish style, but the White Hart is now happily itself again. The partially wooden building between the pub and the Greek Orthodox church is a relic of the old White Hart, to which it was added as an assembly room, perhaps in the late 1830s.

The first White Hart, Church Road, in 1868.

The second White Hart, Church Road, c.1905.

THE WHITE HART TAVERN, NO.367 NORWOOD ROAD

Norwood's other White Hart was founded, and probably built, in 1868 or 1869 by a young man named William Cressell. He appears in an 1870 directory as 'builder, decorator, and contractor, White Hart inn, 9 Thurlow terrace'. In 1868 his building business had been in Thurlow Park Road. This, then, is yet another example of the very close link between the building and innkeeping trades. William Cressell only held the licence for two or three years, but in 1874 Miss Charlotte Cressell appears in his place. She was perhaps a sister, as William Cressell was certainly not old enough to have an adult daughter. The only subsequent landlords to stay for more than a few years were the Oxley Wydells, who ran the White Hart from 1922-45, and Joseph and Gladys Shaw, who were in charge in the 1950s and perhaps later. The White Hart is still in business, as one of the most old-fashioned of the Norwood pubs.

The White
Hart Tavern,
Norwood Road,
c.1910.

THE WHITE LION, SOUTH NORWOOD HILL

The White Lion stood on the east side of South Norwood Hill, opposite Grange Hill. It was Francis Tummons, the Church Road farmer, who granted the original lease of the pub to Henry Southern, probably in 1826. Southern is first listed in the rate books, for a house valued at £15, in April 1827. By February 1829 the description was 'White Lion Public House' and the valuation £21. What is not clear from this is whether Henry Southern built the pub on a fresh site. He may have enlarged one of the existing cottages in this little working class enclave in what was otherwise an exclusive, even an aristocratic, part of Norwood. Southern remained until the early 1830s.

The landlady in 1839, Mary Trowbridge, got into trouble for 'allowing persons to be in the house during the hours of divine service.' She claimed that some were her lodgers and others coachmen who had brought their employers to All Saints' church and put up their horses at the pub while waiting for the service to end, but she was fined £2 plus costs all the same. The most notable of her successors were Stephen Rose from the early 1840s to 1855, and Henry Gillingham from 1855-61. Gillingham was previously at the Holly Bush, and before that probably at the Rising Sun, Spa Hill.

In its last decade, with the original lease expiring in 1871, and little prospect of its being renewed, the White Lion became shabby and disreputable. William Farmer, the Church Road bookseller, was not complimentary about it. After recalling the water trough that stood outside, he continued, 'From my experience of one or two inquests I have had to attend in it, there was none of that freshness and comfort one would expect in such an open position, for it was a very stuffy, frouzy sort of place that I was glad to get out of.' Being at a pub to view a body is not, perhaps, the thing most likely to create cheerful memories, but there is other evidence that all was not well. The next landlord, Edward Frederick Greening, was frequently before the magistrates, for allowing gambling, or when the police had to break up fights. His attempt to produce a better impression on his neighbours was rather bizarre. In 1864, in a 'spacious booth erected in the rear', he hosted a jolly meeting of the Society of Benevolent Brothers, a burial club. The last landlord of the White Lion was John Sowerby, who did nothing to improve the reputation of the house. There were more drunken quarrels, and in 1869 he was accused by the police of Sunday trading, and his licence was only renewed after a severe warning.

The wealthy neighbours had no doubt long been wishing to remove the White Lion and its tumbledown satellites. Their chance came when all the leases expired in 1871. Joseph James Welch of Beaulieu Heights bought the pub and cottages and built three large houses in their place. Or rather he ordered the building of the houses but (allegedly) fell victim to the poisonous vapours released when the cesspits on the site were excavated. His houses survived until the early 1960s. The site of the White Lion is now the lawn in front of Nos 57-70 Dorrington Court.

The White Swan Hotel now Bluebottle, No.79 Westow Hill

The present White Swan (or Bluebottle as it is currently called) is the third building in which the pub has been carried on. The first was one of a pair of semi-detached cottages, converted into a beerhouse in or shortly before 1841. Arthur Saward claimed in 1907 that the pub 'was built upon the site of a smithy kept by a Mr Adams', but I cannot find any trace of a Norwood blacksmith of that name. The 1841 census lists Joseph Preedy as a 'publican' on what appears to be this site. He can probably be identified with the Joseph Preddy (see the Fountain Head) who was a corn & coal merchant and brewer in Crown Lane by 1845. The two spellings of the name long continued to be interchangeable. Next door to Preedy in 1841 was a hackney coachman named William Trundle, so it is likely that the 'William Trundle beer retailer, Westow Hill' who appears in the 1845 directory is the same man, and that he had taken over the White Swan from his neighbour. It was perhaps Trundle's coaching interests that led to the building of a range of stables to the east of the pub, on the Lambeth/Camberwell boundary.

These first two landlords are only probable. Certainty is reached with Benjamin Bockham, who is listed as a beershop keeper at the White Swan (the first appearance of the name) in the 1851 census, and as a beer retailer in Westow Hill in an 1851 directory. He was a very lucky man who chanced to acquire a public house just opposite the Crystal Palace site a year or two before the first whisper of the imminent arrival of the great pleasure dome caused property prices in Upper Norwood to multiply. Elizabeth Dee remembered the pub in 1852 as, 'the picturesque White Hart, which stood back well off the road, with seats in front, and here later, during the construction of the Crystal Palace, often as many as 200 men, principally ground workers, took their meals al fresco.' An 1854 engraving shows a corner of the pub, with an archway beside it leading to the Swan Tea Garden. That was not for the benefit of the navvies, but the visitors to the Crystal Palace who had succeeded them as the pub's best customers.

Two important events in the pub's history must have occurred at about this time. A full licence had been obtained by 1855, when it is referred to as the White Swan Hotel, and the premises were rebuilt on a much larger scale. This may have been the work of Benjamin Bockham, of his successor John Gibbons, who was in charge by 1855, or of Thomas Masters, the licensee by 1860. Masters is perhaps the most likely, as he was an ambitious and extravagant entrepreneur, who was involved with many of the Upper Norwood hotels and pubs at this period.

Above: The second White Swan in 1883.

Left: The third White Swan, *c.*1948, before the loss of the third storey.

Opposite: The third White Swan in 1999.

See the Royal Crystal Palace and Victoria hotels for more about him. This rebuilding confirmed the White Swan as one of the leading inns of Norwood, but it lasted for less than thirty years. By that time there was a growing trend for sprawling pubs to be replaced by taller and more compact 'gin palaces', releasing valuable land for the building of shops alongside. The Woodman and the Jolly Sailor were other local examples. The White Swan received this treatment in the mid-1880s, probably when Charles William Bennett was landlord. The new building created beside it was the London & County Bank. The architect may have been J. Jewhurst.

This third pub on the site is the one that survives, but it was originally a three-storey building, not two as we know it today. It has been said that the loss of the top floor was the result of

bomb damage, but it can certainly not have been a direct or immediate result, as various 1950s photographs show the pub intact. The demolition of the top floor must have been carried out towards the end of the long reign of Hugh Taylor as landlord, from 1933 until his death in 1966. Taylor, 'had a very large picture of Winston Churchill in the bar and would not serve you if you were sporting a red tie!' With his passing there began an unhappy period for the pub, when there was frequent trouble with the police over unlicenced strip shows, fights, etc. After a long closure in 2000 the poor old White Swan emerged with its present ugly colour and name.

THE WILLIAM STANLEY, NOS 7 AND 8 SOUTH NORWOOD HIGH STREET

The group of shops of which the pub now forms a part was probably built in the 1880s on the site of a terrace of private houses known as South Place. For a year or so before the birth of the William Stanley the premises were used for a very dubious-looking eatery called the Tramshed, of which the only attractive feature was the array of tram photographs scattered around the walls. Perhaps it was this display that suggested to the Wetherspoon scouts that the building might be suitable for one of their pubs. That enterprising chain opened its South Norwood branch here early in 1999, and had the happy thought of naming it after the suburb's great benefactor, whose other local monuments — his factory, his first house, even his school — were vanishing or under threat. Although the High Street was already so lavishly supplied with pubs, this one has been a popular addition, and has not so far put any of the others out of business.

Left: The William Stanley in 1999.

Opposite: The first Woodman, *c.*1867.

THE WOODMAN HOTEL, NO.56 WESTOW HILL

The Woodman, one of the great inns of Norwood, was founded between 1816 and 1819, in August of which year 'Mr Rose, the sign of the Woodman, Norwood' is mentioned in an advertisement. He was William Rose, the owner, who remained the landlord until 1834. The original pub was a low, rambling building with a forecourt, directly opposite Woodland Road. Behind were gardens featuring a skittle ground and other rural delights, and also, as this was one of the points of call for the Norwood coaches, a large range of stabling. It was called the Woodman Inn & Coach Office in 1838. After William Rose the most important name in the history of the original Woodman is Jeffrey. James Jeffrey was landlord from 1847-53, and his widow Maria until 1865. The stables, which had greatly increased in size and importance after the arrival of the Crystal Palace, were under the management of Alfred Jeffrey until long after the family had given up the pub. An 1855 advertisement proclaimed, 'Crystal Palace - visitors will find the Old Woodman Tavern the most comfortable and best conducted house near London. The Crystal Palace Company's splendid range of stabling for 500 horses, with a private entrance to the house, at the back.'

Maria Jeffrey tried to sell the lease and goodwill of the Woodman in 1856. It was described as:

The celebrated Woodman Inn, Norwood, together with the immense range of stabling for 400 horses, erected at an outlay of many thousand pounds, and at present on lease to the Palace Company. The house itself has been entirely remodelled to suit the large and increasing trade. The lease of the whole has nearly 70 years unexpired. The rent is reduced by underletting the stables to the Company to a nominal ground rent. This important property is too well-known to need much description. The large trade hitherto done must be still further increased, the ground opposite having been let for building 100 houses and shops, the exclusive trade coming to the Woodman, no tavern, beer-shop, or stabling being allowed on any part of the estate.

This attributes very little initiative to the future residents of Woodland Road and district, who would have to walk only a short distance left or right to find alternative pubs in Westow Hill, not to mention the ones available in Gipsy Hill.

The next important figure after the Jeffreys had only a very brief connection with the Woodman, but a crucially damaging one. George Edward Williams, who cannot have been landlord for more than a year, applied for a renewal of his licence in March 1876. His solicitor explained that 'as an ancient inn its rooms were inconveniently low, and it was altogether unsuited to modern requirements. Mr Williams had therefore considerably altered and improved it … at a considerable expense', but had neglected to submit the plans to the Bench. The magistrates' main concern was that a skating rink 'was being constructed contiguous to the Woodman, indeed on a portion of the Woodman premises', but when they were assured that Mr Williams had nothing to do with it they granted the renewal. 'Considerably altered and improved' was a diplomatic understatement. The inn had been completely rebuilt.

The second Woodman, *c.*1948.

As happened at the Jolly Sailor in South Norwood, the new Woodman was a sadly prosaic substitute for the picturesque original, with nothing to distinguish it from the adjoining shops, so that except for its historic associations with the early history of the Triangle, it is hard to regret its loss. The new pub did not inspire its landlords with much loyalty. Williams left as soon as his destructive work was done. The longest-serving of his successors was William Frederick Langdon from 1914-1924. The last was R.J. Ellum, after 1958. On 11 January 1963 a local paper reported that 'the long-disused public house, The Woodman, Westow Hill, went under the hammers of demolition men this week'. The restaurant known as Joanna's is now on the site.

BIBLIOGRAPHY

ANDERSON, J. Corbet – *The Great North Wood, with a description ... of Upper, West, and South Norwood* (1898; New York 1932).

BRANDWOOD, Geoff, *et al* – *Licenced to Sell: the History and Heritage of the Public House* (2004).

BROWNE, Rupert Montague - Notes on Norwood, 1917 (manuscript).

CHEESEMAN, Beryl D. – *Treetops and Terraces: a bygone era of New Town, Upper Norwood*, SE19 (1991).

CHEESEMAN, Beryl D. – *Treetops and Terraces - and the walls came a-tumbling down: New Town, Upper Norwood*, SE19 (1994).

DEE, Mrs Elizabeth Louisa – *Memories of Norwood since 1852* (n.d. – *c.*1908?); G. Lucas, Bethnal Green.

DUDMAN, Jill – *Brixton and Norwood in Old Photographs* (1995).

The *Estates Gazette Year Book of Auction Sales, 1892-1921*.

FARMER, William – *Bygone Day's [sic] in Norwood*, by the Editor of *The Norwood Review*, a series of nine articles published between 4 Feb 1888 and 20 July 1889.

FLANAGAN, Bob – *West Norwood Cemetery's Sportsmen* (1995).

FROST, Thomas – *Reminiscences of a Country Journalist* (1886, new ed. 1888).

GENT, John, and Tom Samson - *Croydon from Above* (1999).

GREENWOOD, Christopher – *Surrey Described*, being an enumeration of the seats and residences of the nobility, clergy, and gentry (1823).

JOHNSON, May (ed.) – *Talking of Croydon 3: South Norwood 1892-1992* (Croydon Oral History Society, 1992).

MAUDSLAY, Alfred Percival – *Life in the Pacific Fifty Years Ago* (1930).

The Norwood Review (journal of The Norwood Society), 1960 to date.

PHILLIPS, W.T. – *Norwood in Days of Old: the personal recollections of an old inhabitant,* reprinted from the *Norwood Press* (1912).

SALTER, Brian – *Retracing Canals to Croydon and Camberwell* (1986).

SAWARD, Arthur A. *et al* (published J.A. Squire) – *Picturesque Norwood, 3rd.ed.* (1907).

Sydenham, Dulwich, and Norwood: a handy guide to rambles in the district (T. Fisher Unwin's *Half-Holiday Handbooks* 1881).

The Times, (1785 to date).

WALKER, Peter – *Croydon and Its Pubs: 1, A Brief History* (1999); *2, A Century of Pubs and Publicans* 1839-1939 (2001).

WILSON, J.B. (prepared by H.A. Wilson) – *The Story of Norwood* (1973); revised edition (1990).

List of Alternative Pub Names and Nicknames

Aldwinckle's see the Thurlow Arms
Black Sheep see the Queen's Arms, Westow Hill
Bluebottle see the White Swan
Bug & Bolster see the Crown
Cherry Tree see South Norwood Railway Hotel
Cintra House Hotel see the Star Hotel
Crown & Anchor see also the Royal Albert
Crown Coffee Palace see the Alexandra Hotel
Crystal Palace Inn see the Royal Crystal Palace Hotel
Crystal Tower see the Royal Albert
Gipsy House see Old Gipsy House and the Gipsy Tavern
Gold Coast see the Spread Eagle
Harvester see The Beulah Spa
Holborn Bars see the Queen's Arms, Westow Hill
Jack Beards at the Palace see the Royal Crystal Palace Hotel
Jack Stamps see the Thurlow Arms
Lion see the Victoria Hotel
London Stores see the London Tavern
Mansion see the Paxton Tavern
Mill see the Royal Albert
Mollard's Grand Hotel see the Park Hotel
Occasional Half see the Royal Crystal Palace Hotel
Oceans Apart see the Prince of Denmark
Old Gipsy House see also the Gipsy Tavern
Old Gipsy Queen see the Gipsy Tavern
Old Holborn Bars see the Queen's Arms, Westow Hill
Old Top Hat see the Fox and Hounds

O'Neill's see the White Hart
Orange Kipper see the Queen's Arms, Westow Hill
Palace see the Royal Crystal Palace Hotel
Palace Hotel and Tavern see the Paxton Tavern
Pheasant see the Spread Eagle
Pickled Newt see the Albert Tavern
Pleasant Pheasant see the Spread Eagle
Portmanor see the Signal Hotel
Princess Alexandra see the Alexandra Hotel
Quality Hotel see the Queen's Hotel
Queen's Head see the Queen's Arms, Portland Road
Railway Signal see the Signal Hotel
Rat see Victoria Arms
Red Lion see the Victoria Hotel
Roaring Donkey see the Castle
Rockwell's see Los Toreros
Royal Beulah Spa Tea Gardens see the Rambler's Rest
Royal Hotel see the Beulah Spa Hotel
Royal Sailor see the Jolly Sailor
Southern Pride see the King's Head
Sportsman see the Royal Crystal Palace Hotel
Star and Garter see the Star Hotel
Swan see the White Swan
Tramshed see the William Stanley
Two Bobbys see the Queen's Arms, Portland Road
White Hart see also the Jolly Sailor
William IV see George IV (1 and 2)
Windmill see the Royal Albert
Ye Old Gipsy House see the Gipsy Tavern

Index of Landlords and Proprietors

INDEX